Janey

You Never Realise

Jane. A. Anderson

ISBN 979-8-9882981-0-6

LEGAL DISCLAIMER

The entire content of ("Janey You Never Realise"), must be considered as exclusively informative and cannot in any way be understood as a substitute, alternative or supplementary of professional opinions or medical consultations, nor refer to specific individual cases, for which we invite you to consult your own attending physician and / or recognized specialists.

The contents of ("Janey You Never Realise") are for informational purposes only and should not be intended to treat, diagnose, prevent or treat any ailment or disease. The author of this work declines any responsibility for any consequences deriving from a use of its contents other than merely informative. Nothing contained in this work constitutes or intends to constitute a suggestion of any nature. If the user of ("Janey You Never Realise") if you feel the need for advice in relation to any topic, you are invited to contact a qualified professional in the specific field.

If the user ("Janey You Never Realise") suspects or is aware of having or having had or being exposed to problems, disturbances and / or physical or psychological illnesses and in any case in any case, must rely on appropriate medical treatment recommended by a professional of their own trust.

Despite the scrupulous care used in the preparation of ("Janey You Never Realise"), drawn up with the utmost accuracy and diligence, it is not possible ensure that the information contained within it is free from errors, omissions or inaccuracies.

(JANE ANN ANDERSON "Janey You Never Realise" THE AUTHOR) disclaim any liability, direct and indirect, towards readers, regarding inaccuracies, errors, omissions, damages, deriving from the aforementioned contents.

The author of ("Janey You Never Realise") cannot guarantee the users of the book to obtain the same results of personal, character growth, psychological, motivational, physical or any other nature or denomination on a par with as set out in this work.

Within ("Janey You Never Realise") the ideas of consultants and experts are cited and hosted which in an absolutely free form, not constituting what they affirmed an opinion of a professional or similar nature, offered their contribution for information purposes only, without any presumption or willingness to place oneself above the recognized traditional medical system. It is at the free discretion of the user of ("Janey You Never Realise") and its absolute responsibility for any willingness to follow or replicate some of the advice proposed therein or to contact other competent personnel, according to your own beliefs, knowledge, habits and wills.

Everything included within ("Janey You Never Realise") must always be understood as the subjective opinion of the author, given that these considerations can also run counter to the precepts of knowledge taught in universities and / or in the scientific world and therefore go there considered as simple expressions or controversies of a personal and in any case non-professional nature, having to make exclusive reference to/and reliance solely on traditional and recognized fields of knowledge.

Reviews

Jane's debut novel is a delightful recollection of growing up on a farm in Northumberland. Illustrating how farming and the countryside shaped the whole family and communities' lives, "You never realise" is filled with gentle humour. A compassionate tale of Jane and her brother developing a strong work ethic and treating animals and the land with respect.

Hillary Micklemas

"Jane captures your attention from the very beginning. Her story is so mesmerising that you can't help but get lost amongst the pages. She captures the events in impeccable detail and actuates your emotions.

This is a book you're not going to want to put down! I can't wait to read more from this amazing author!"

Laura Berggren, Best Selling Author and Publisher & Health and Wellness Coach

"A heart warming and engaging canter through the joyful times of youth. Honestly written from the pen of a skilled author, this is a book to snuggle up with."

Frances Alice Headley

"I have learnt so much reading this delightful book who knew life on a farm was so busy. The detailed descriptions bring it all to life."

Sian Jones

"I loved every page of this book. I experienced Jane's emotions as I read. Can't recommend it enough."

Victoria Springer

Love Letter for you my reader

My inner me finds me having to put pen to paper to tell you how much I am in love with you my reader.

I write this from my heart, my inner me, from deep down inside.

My love for you all is unreal and having not written a letter of love before this is a whole new experience. You all make my life worth living and I look forward to many years of filling your life too.

You complete me as a person and I love to share experiences be it positive or negative so we can live the joy together but also live the hard times too and make those a little easier for us both.

Life is for living and I would love for you all to enjoy living life with me.

Words of love don't flow easy to me so after the traumas of the past few years so I hope you find the essence and feelings I have for you my reader in this letter.

My books are all written with love for you all in the hope you too can find inner peace with yourselves.

J

♥

Table of Content

Foreword

This is the start of my journey as an author and my increasing awareness of me.

If the last three years have taught me anything, it's that life, as we know it, is too short. Live for today, as tomorrow is never promised.

Finding solace in mentorship, to give me direction and focus, I found release in writing 'Janey You Never Realise.

For me, it was a trip down memory lane, a deep delve to the inner me that needed to be exposed, and enjoyed, in equal measure. A journey of growth in a short space of time, and a tale of childhood that had all, but been forgotten.

A chance to relive some amazing memories of my early years, incorporating life on the farm and the teachings that you never realise at the time.

Jane.A.Anderson

Dedication

For me

Introduction

"Welcome to my world" said Jane to no one in particular. This seemed to be an increasing habit, especially whilst out walking the dogs, Bella the black and white Springer Spaniel and Mollie the Collie. Jane had heard dogs were good listeners and the good thing was, they didn't answer back. After a big sigh, which seemed to be a regular occurrence, Jane continued her daily walk, talking to herself occasionally as she went.

"Hey ho, life is life and well, something will happen, something will get sorted."

"Life will be good eventually."

"Time is a good healer."

The wind and rain didn't help Jane's mood, it was blowing a hooley and she was soaked through. But the dogs were enjoying their run around the fields of the family farm in the hills of Northumberland. On the plus side, thankfully there was nobody to hear Jane's ramblings as some days they were unrepeatable. It is a daily ritual to let it all out whilst walking and some days feel better than others.

There is so much to love in the countryside and Jane looks for as much of the good as she can. On a sunny frosty morning, in the depths of winter, it is astonishing to see the cobwebs on the bracken bushes and is a true-life form, many photos of these have been taken over the years. Being positive is a struggle currently for Jane and her mind is so jumbled. Life has been tough; a challenge and some days she just doesn't know how she is able to function. The last three years have seen a dramatic change to the life that Jane was living.

"Life is life, and we take the rough with the smooth. Over the last three years, life has thrown some huge curve balls at me." Jane continued her ramblings "This has been hard, what is normal life, it seems like a lifetime ago."

Rewind 50 years and a beautiful baby girl was brought into the world, a 'Thursday's child has far to go' and how right that turned out to be.

Chapter 1

'It's the journey and who you become'

-Ciaran Deaney

Travelling back in time to a world without worry...........

Little Jane woke up in her tiny, but cosy bedroom, yawned and stretched. The cosy little room was her safe space and she loved it. The sun was shining through the curtains and today was going to be a good day, or was it? Life was good most days, but school was just school, how could other children say that they enjoy it?

"You two moving up there?" came the voice of her Mum from downstairs. Thomas, Jane's younger brother, was obviously as excited as she was to be getting up for school. They would both rather be helping out at home; it was lambing time on the farm and there was always plenty to do, fetching and carrying water, as well as feed, or even feeding the pet lambs.

It was Thursday, so only today and tomorrow, and then they could get totally immersed into helping out over the weekend.

From a young age, they had been involved with all aspects of the farm and they both loved being part of it. The fun of being allowed to wander freely and explore was a gift to growing up on the farm. All their friends were extremely jealous that they had this huge playground to experience, although at times Jane didn't see it that way. Friends were always keen to offer to help out, just so they could enjoy the freedom that Jane and Thomas had on a daily basis.

Jane and Thomas made it down for breakfast just in the nick of time to grab a quick bowl of cereal, before jumping into the car to make the short trip up the road to school. Mum at the wheel as always, Dad didn't have time, as he had all his daily jobs to do. Mum waved them both off at the school gates "have fun today kids" her usual comment.

No doubt she'd be stood there for half an hour chatting to the other Mums, or maybe stop at the post office to chat to her old school friend Chris, the postmaster, it was almost a ritual to stop off at the Post Office and get 'something'. I am sure that it was just an excuse to catch up on the village gossip, but on reflection, it did mean that we got a 10p mix up. Regular as clockwork if we had been out anywhere 'Oh I had better stop to see if Chris has those nice cakes in' mum would say, or 'we need some bread before Harry (the baker van) calls on Friday.' Chris always made us laugh and always added extra sweets to our bags. Chris and Mum had also gone to the village school and were lifelong friends.

Today was a good day as Jane and Thomas had been told they could walk home from school on their own, mum normally met them at the school gates, but not today. Mum would be helping Dad with lambing jobs, so it meant they both felt quite grown up. It also meant they too could call at the Post Office, or the shop, and get sweets, bonus!

School was school, and neither Jane nor Thomas actually enjoyed it, but the day passed quickly and they were soon dashing out the school gates. They passed all the waiting Mums, all waving and saying hello to them, but neither of them paid any attention, they were focused on one thing and one thing only, sweets and, maybe, a passing thought to being allowed to help out when they got home. They started their first solo walk from school feeling extremely proud of themselves, they could do this. Their first chance of independence and a chance to visit the shops without Mum, or Grandma, as the saying goes 'like kids in a sweetie shop'!

"Should we stop at the shop or the Post Office?" Thomas asked, with a cheeky grin on his face.

“I don’t mind either.” replied Jane, not being too bothered, just thinking sweets.

“Let’s do the Post Office.” said Thomas.

They quickened their pace and made it to the Post Office in record time. It was a good thing that, although the village is only small, they had the choice of having both a Post Office and a shop.

The bell on the door rang out as they entered the Post Office. Chris was behind the counter and gave them both a raised eyebrow look.

“Hello you two, now I wonder what you are after?” he questioned knowingly. Jane and Thomas looked at each other and laughed, were they that predictable?

“A 10p mix up please” said Jane, “Oh, with a white mouse for Penny the dog.”

“Coming up, do you want to choose?” questioned Chris “No, you choose” smiled Jane.

Chris handed Jane her sweets in the little white paper bag.

“Now then Thomas, what you after?” asked Chris “the same, but no mouse for Penny, I’ll have one for me. Oh and just put them on Grandma’s paper bill” replied Thomas.

They all laughed, poor Grandma got stung for all their sweets and treats at the Post Office, but it was never an issue, as her only grandchildren, they were spoilt rotten.

They waved bye to Chris and headed down the steep bank home. Both laughing and giggling, they were paying no attention to the world around them, just eating their sweets as they went. Maybe this was the way forward, sweets every night on the way home from school. Their laughter was short lived, as Mum had been expecting them straight home, although they thought she knew where they had been.

"Get your wellies on, and we'll head out and feed the sheep in the pens, to help out Dad." said Mum "Oh, and put those sweet bags in the bin, if you're finished." So, she did know. How do Mums always know? Jane and Thomas were sure Mum had some kind of radar, or tracking device on them.

Chapter 2

'If it's not planted properly, it won't grow'

-Brian Cassidy

Wellies and old coats on, they headed out the door, to the shed across the yard. There was lots of blaring from the sheep, as they saw the cake bag. Thomas went straight to get the wheelbarrow, to help push this round, to feed the small pens where a ewe, who had lambed already, was put with her lambs. This was to allow the ewe time to bond with the lambs, away from the other ewes.

There were no mini wheelbarrows when Jane and Thomas were small, so they took a handle each and pushed it round the pens, often getting stuck in the straw bedding, but having a good giggle as they went. Their sandcastle building buckets made a great scoop to fill the pen buckets with cake. It was also a good excuse to buy new ones when they went away on their annual holiday. Once the pens all had cake, Jane and Thomas had to tootle off and get water. Well, we all know what happens when kids get hold of a hose pipe! As per usual Thomas was first there and yep, you've guessed it, soaked Jane through. This was all part of the fun! It also meant that Thomas had to water the pens, while Jane went into the house, with Mum, to jump into a nice warm bath - method in her madness.

Lambing time is a tough time of year in the farming calendar. Many farmers wouldn't want to work out the hours that they actually work in this period. Weather plays a huge part in the lambing process, as some farms lamb all their sheep outdoors. The family were lucky and had shed space to lamb inside, but this also comes with its difficulties. There is no right or wrong way, and it comes to pass that the last ewe to lamb is always a celebration. The welcoming of new life onto the farm is a gift, which Jane and Thomas, as children, didn't fully appreciate at the time.

The weekend soon came after another day at school, Mum at the wheel, dropping Jane and Thomas off, waving them off and then being there to collect them later.

"You two had a good day?" said Mum.

"Well, it's the weekend and that's another week of school over." said Thomas. Even at first school, Thomas was counting the days until he could actually leave school.

"Are we helping tonight?" Jane asked.

"Yes, we have some pet lambs for you to feed tonight." said Mum.

The pet lambs are always so cute, but Jane and Thomas were always taught never to get too attached, as they might get a new mummy. Jane knew that there were teachings from a very young age, about death too, as not all the lambs survive. The pet lambs were often adopted onto the ewes who had lost a lamb. The hardest part was if one of our beloved pet lambs didn't make it. This has probably helped Jane throughout her life deal with grief, as it has been a way of life, albeit not on the human front. Farm kids are resilient in many ways, and this is just one, there will be others that come to the fore.

Jane and Thomas were into the house at breakneck speed, to get their waterproofs and wellies on, all while Mum mixed the milk into bottles to feed the pet lambs. Off they all went - bottles tucked into their jackets to keep the milk warm. Mum had already fed the lambs at lunchtime, so the lambs knew when Jane and Thomas popped their heads over the pen, which was made out of small straw bales, that they were going to get fed.

"I want to feed the black one. It's so tiny like a soft toy." Jane said.

"That's fine" said Mum "Thomas can feed the speckled one."

"I think we should give them names; I'm going to call mine Menace!" Thomas was an avid Beano fan at the time, probably the only thing he has read from cover to cover.

"Well, I'm calling mine Blackie" said Jane, how original. So, the pet lambs had been named. As it was nearing the end of lambing time, Mum said this would be ok, as it wasn't likely that they would get a new mummy. So, Jane and Thomas would have to look after them until they were able to join the rest of the flock.

Jane and Thomas set about feeding the lambs and it didn't take long for both the lambs to have full tummies.

"How was school today?" asked Dad, who seemed to appear from nowhere.

"OK." Jane and Thomas both responded.

"Jolly good, well I'm just about done, do you want to come and check the last of the lambers with me, and Mum can get the tea sorted?" said Dad.

Off they went to the big shed, to look at the last of the lambers and all was calm. In the other pen, the older lambs were having races up and down, while the ewes settled down for the night.

Jane and Thomas got back to the house, stripped off the waterproofs and dumped them in the usual heap in the utility. After a quick bath, they sat down to stew and mash, just what was required after a busy day at school and helping out. The family all had some fire time in the room. It was good to get some time with Dad, as he'd been extra busy with lambing and the only time that Jane and Thomas had seen him was when they were outside helping, even if he did fall asleep in the cosy room.

The weekend flew over, Jane and Thomas were outside helping for most of it. There was ewes and lambs to take out to the fields, to settle into their new environment of being outside, the next step after the shed. Menace and Blackie continued to grow. It gave Thomas and Jane an added interest and also taught them that farm animals are solely dependent on them, as human beings, to care for them. Jane and Thomas were up every morning before school to feed their pet lambs, and it was the first job when they got home on an evening. Jane and Thomas felt like they had a purpose and at a young age, got used to the responsibility of caring.

Lambing time was soon over for another year, but Menace and Blackie continued to keep Jane and Thomas occupied. As the days got brighter and the weather became kinder, the lambs moved into the small field opposite the house. This small field was the drying green as it was, where Mum hung out the washing.

Thomas and Jane built a little shed out of some old tin sheets, on the drying green, so that their much-loved lambs had a small shelter. They were sure Dad did some work on the shed when they weren't there, but the thought was there, and in their heads it was perfect. The lambs soon grew and no longer needed their daily milk, they were soon eating the fresh green grass that was growing in the spring sunshine. They did get a little bit of cake to help them along, and as soon as they got stronger, they were allowed to join the main flock of sheep. That was a tough day, seeing them run out of the yard, with the rest of the flock, no longer needing Jane and Thomas to look after them. It was funny though if Jane and Thomas ever went to check the sheep, with Dad, their pet lambs would always find them.

With the pressures and tiredness of lambing soon behind, the farming calendar continues. There is no real quiet time on a farm, as there is always something to do.

Lambing time was always, in Jane's eyes, the start of the farming year, as it is bringing new life into the world. And Springtime, with the snowdrops and daffodils shooting up in places that you would never expect.

Easter was always a cause for celebration! And no, not just because they got a heap of chocolate eggs, but Jane and Thomas got to spend time with family and friends. Easter Sunday was spent with Grandma and Granda (Mum's parents), who lived literally next door, along the yard.

Jane and Thomas spent a great deal of time with Grandma and Granda, as they could just walk next door. Grandma and Granda lived in the original farmhouse, which was, to Jane and Thomas at the time, massive. A proper old-fashioned house, which at one time, had servant's quarters and huge rooms to entertain in. The servant's quarters in the attic, consisted of three rooms and the signorial bells were still hanging on the walls. The views from the windows across the valley were amazing.

It wasn't until Jane and Thomas were a little older that that they ventured up the stairs to the attic, but wow, what a place for adventures. It was like having your own house to explore, although it was a bit spooky at times. Jane loved to play with her Mum's old dolls house up there, and rummage through the numerous big wooden trunks of stuff. Some of it, Jane and Thomas had no clue what it was! But it gave way to hearing some great stories of when their grandparents were younger, and the tough times that they had endured in their life, to get to where they were.

Granda's Father had changed his name, by deed poll, to purchase the family farm. There were also the pictures of family in Australia. Granda loved to tell the story of his grandfather getting on a boat to Australia, to make a new life for his family in Perth.

Granda Tom, as Jane and Thomas called him, was great fun and a fabulous storyteller. Jimmy mouse was born during one coffee time, spent in the big house.

"Thomas, have you been in the fridge?" asked Granda.

Thomas raised his eyebrows "What?"

"The fridge, I think there's something living in there" said Granda.

Well, as kids, you take anything that an adult says as the truth, it is how we learn what life is, with open minds to receive.

Granda continued "Jimmy mouse lives in there, did you not know? He's the one that turns the light on and off."

Granda looked at Jane and Thomas over the kitchen table, they were both intrigued, so he continued. "You can't see him obviously, as he hides when you open the door, but he's there, he goes off on his adventures when we are busy"

"What kind of adventures?" Jane asked

"Oh, all sorts. He often pops down to the river, to see his friends down there."

Jane and Thomas looked at each other and smiled "Who are his friends?" asked Thomas.

"Well, there's Harry hare, Rebecca rabbit, Sally snail and Milly mouse."

And so, Jimmy mouse was born. Jane and Thomas spent endless hours listening to Granda tell his tales, which looking back, all had an impact on their learning of nature and its ways. Jane and Thomas looked for Jimmy mouse's friends when they were out for walks to the river, or up the Lłonnen, with Grandma, often making tales of their own. They often looked in the tree trunks and tree roots to see if these could be homes for Jimmy's friends.

The river was a huge draw when Jane and Thomas were children, but they were continually warned of the dangers of swimming in the river, with the whirlpools, and stories of people who had got into difficulty whilst swimming. With it just being a short walk from the house, but over a railway crossing, it was a while before Jane and Thomas were allowed to go to throw stones unaccompanied.

Life was good in the world of little Jane. And the farming year continued, it never stops, it is a cycle of life and growth, as our life is. Springtime is the new life and Jane always classed this as the start of the faming year, not January, as January is just a continuation of feeding and looking after animals through the winter months.

Jane thought of lambing as the start of the big jobs in the farming cycle, with new life being brought into the world to show for all the hardwork

Chapter 3

'If you think you can't, think that you can. Your thinking is the only thing stopping you'

-Ciaran Deaney

School always seemed to be an added complication to living on the farm, although both Jane and Thomas went on a daily basis. There always seemed to be something more exciting happening at home, whilst they were at school. This was probably not the case, as it would be the usual day to day jobs of farming life, but in Little Jane's eyes it was so much easier being a farmer, than studying at school. As Jane and Thomas were told on numerous occasions "Do you two think I just sit here and drink coffee all day?" Dad would say. They wouldn't find out for themselves until they entered the world of work. How wrong they were!

The potato planting was always a fun job to watch, and as Jane and Thomas grew, they got a chance to sit on the machine on the back of the tractor and plop the potatoes down the shoot, to be buried in the ground to grow. It was actually quite a stressful job, they had to concentrate and not miss a holder. These would be harvested in October half term. They were planted in the fields over the railway, in the sandy soil, next to the river, fabulous soil for growing. Although not great if the river happened to flood.

The ewes and lambs continue to graze in the fields, and the corn crops start to sprout. Mum continued her daily "You two up yet?" Jane and Thomas quickly getting dressed and grabbing a bowl of cereal, then take them to school and pick them up. Jane and Thomas had a lovely local village school, with friends from the village, which was an added bonus, as everyone was in walking distance. It was a bit harder for Jane and Thomas, as they didn't live directly in the village, to be able to go and call on friends after school. Mum did well to distract them most nights from the 'can we go and play in the village' question.

"You two fancy a walk across to see how Dad is getting on?" said Mum

"Need to finish watching this programme first" would be the reply from both Jane and Thomas.

Wellies or old trainers on, they would head out for a walk when the weather was good, always closely followed by Penny, the Golden Labrador.

"Keep up will you," said Mum

"Just checking the feeders are full" came an echoey voice from the lamb creep.

"Get out of there - your new trousers will end up with holes, like the last ones." replied Mum.

They all ended up in fits of giggles as Thomas emerged on hands and knees, closely followed by Menace and Blackie, the pet lambs, they followed us across the field, until we climbed the style into the next field.

"They still remember us." Jane said.

"Yes, they'll always remember you because you looked after them when they were small and gave them love." replied Mum.

"They'll be useful to help get the sheep in when they're older" commented Thomas.

"Hmmm maybe they will" said Mum, not too confidently.

"There's Dad in the tractor, he's spreading fertiliser to help the grass grow" Jane said.

"Looks like he's nearly finished," said Thomas.

Jane and Thomas both waved, and Dad gave them a thumbs up from the tractor cab. Penny had found the water trough to jump into, to cool down and was very happy with herself, tail wagging as she came over to stand with them at the field gate. All of a sudden, she decided to shake and they were all covered. Not all water troughs are clean, especially when there is no livestock drinking from them on a regular basis.

"Argh great" shouted Thomas "I'm not going to be able to wear my favourite trousers for school again tomorrow, they're all mud splattered"

"I'm soaked too" said Jane "Me too," said Mum

"Let's head back and have a nice hot bath before tea." said Mum.

"But I wanted to ride in the tractor," said a very disappointed Thomas

"Another time, let's see if we can find Jimmy mouse on our way home." said Mum.

They headed back slowly, giving Grandma and Granda a wave as they walked past their huge garden.

Bath complete, and with a hearty mince and dumplings in their tummies, Jane and Thomas headed to bed, ready to get a good night sleep, before school again tomorrow. Dad took longer than they thought to get finished, as the tractor had a problem, that he'd had to fix before he got the field finished. Farmers tend to be mechanics, as well as many other things. Then he had his horses to feed, Lady and Beauty. Lady was due to foal at any time, and he was keeping a close eye on her. He popped up to kiss Jane and Thomas both goodnight, and promised Thomas that he would get a ride in the tractor the next time that they were out.

The days passed and the nights started to get lighter, whilst most people love this, it also means that the farmer works longer hours. More light to work outside. The grass and crops keep on growing, and as Spring makes way for summer, the jobs increase.

At weekends, Jane and Thomas would help out to the best of their ability, although being small was never a barrier. They also spent time building dens, with their friends, or just the two of them.

"You coming out to play in the shed? Granda's put up a new swing." said Thomas.

"Oh really, yes I'll be out soon" Jane replied.

The shed that had been used in lambing time, had now been cleaned out, in preparation for the hay and straw to be stored, once harvested. This made a great space for Jane and Thomas to use as a playground. Granda's swing was the best - a rope hanging from the rafters, with proper swing seat that Granda had made. Jane and Thomas spent hours taking turns, often falling out about who had had the longest go.

Learning to ride a bike was like a key to independence and both Jane and Thomas spent hours practicing with their bikes, in the yard between their house and the big house. Granda was always on hand to pick them up and help them back on. While Grandma was keen to feed Jane and Thomas all the treats that they weren't allowed at home. It was great to have Grandma and Granda so close, and Jane and Thomas would stay some nights, and play cards in front of the fire, oh and the added bonus of the heated blankets.

Jane still recalls the old tin tray table that folded out to be used as the card table. It was still a bit spooky going past the attic stairs to the bathroom mind, even as Jane and Thomas got older.

Sometimes Jimmy mouse made an appearance. Jane and Thomas both had their own rooms and had stories with Grandma in bed the next morning. Not as good as the Jimmy mouse stories though, or so they thought. She loved to tell us about when she was a young girl and used to ride her pony, she was quite a horsewoman in her day. One of her favourite stories was telling us about how proud she was of Granda riding in a point to point, amateur racing over jumps, on his horse called Spartan. "You've probably come across his jockey colours in those big chests in the attic"

"Oh are they blue and white?" I asked "Yes that's them, they'll be in amongst all the leather bridles and other bits" said Grandma

"Do you have photos of Granda racing?" asked Thomas.

"No," replied Grandma "but can you remember seeing the silver cups in the china cabinet in the dining room?" She was met with silence, Jane and Thomas had probably seen these on numerous occasions, but not asked what they were, just thinking they were for decoration. "We'll have a look after breakfast," said Grandma. Well that certainly got us moving, how exciting, Granda had won a cup like a hero.

After a special breakfast of porridge, made with cream and heaped with sugar, Grandma's always make a special breakfast. Jane and Thomas raced literally along the hallway to the dining room, which in itself was a huge room, with the table being able to sit at least sixteen with ease.

"There you go" Grandma pointed "The Tynedale Cup for Maiden Race winner."

"Can we hold it?" said Thomas "Of course, let's get the key from the sideboard and open up the cabinet."

Thomas was straight in there and held it aloft. "I'm pretending Newcastle has won the FA cup and I scored the winning goal" Grandma and Jane looked at each other and giggled.

"What's all the giggling in here?" asked Granda as his head popped round the door "Oh I see you've found my cup, I won that on Spartan."

"Yes, Grandma has told us - you must be really good." Jane said, still smiling as Thomas started running round the table chanting "We won the cup, we won the cup!"

"I don't think I could do it now as I was super dooper fit then, but it was an amazing feeling" said Granda "And we were all so proud of him" added Grandma.

Thomas was still lifting the cup up and down chanting, "Well son, we all have to have dreams and goals, let's hope that they come true for you." said Granda.

Thomas did eventually let Jane have a hold of the cup and what an awesome feeling it was, knowing her Granda had won this. It made Jane proud and she carried that feeling with her, and the words about having dreams and goals in life. Jane and Thomas popped the cup back in its pride of place in the centre of the china cabinet, and started looking at all the other bits and pieces.

The silver tea service always caught Jane's eye and she honestly didn't think that it ever got used. Until Jane was in the house one day, dropping off some shopping that they had got for Grandma. The solicitor was there to sort paperwork and there it was, in all its glory, set out on the coffee table in the drawing room, with the sun pouring through the bay windows reflection off the teapot, it looked amazing. Jane was speechless that it was being used, but it was always a special occasion when the solicitor visited.

The Big House was Jane and Thomas's second home growing up, and Jane was grateful for the time that they had with Grandma and Granda. As small kids, they weren't really aware of the whole situation of the generations working together. This became more apparent as they got older and they were often told "Don't go along the yard today, things aren't great at the minute, give it a few days", which was always met with a groan from Jane and Thomas. It is only now Jane realised how hard it was for Mum and Dad, working alongside Granda, who owned the business and really wasn't that open to new suggestions and ideas for moving forward. You could say things don't change, but that's a whole different story.

These little fall outs were resolved around the kitchen table at coffee time, and life on the farm would continue. Dad often said it was hard for him, moving from his family home to come and work alongside Granda, as the farmer.

May is a good month as it is Jane's birthday, usually falling on the first May bank holiday. Jane never had any big parties, but it was always a special day, with friends for tea and Mum's home baking. Everyone loved Mums' caramel shortbread, and this was often a good swap at the packed lunch table, for a chocolate biscuit. Mum also turned her hand to make special cakes, with a hedgehog, with chocolate button spikes being one, and obviously a tractor cake for Thomas.

As littlies, Jane and Thomas often went for a walk to the far side around Jane's birthday, with Grandma, as inevitably Dad would be working during the day. We were sometimes lucky to see the beautiful bluebells, if the spring weather had been kind, their intricate bell-shaped flowers always fascinating. They didn't have a strong scent, but Jane did wonder if it's similar to that of a lily, as these are one of her go to flowers now. Jane and Thomas spent hours sitting amongst them and looking back across to the farm, surveying the fields and catching a glimpse of the tractors working, ploughing and cultivating the ground, ready to plant the crops to harvest later in the year.

May Bank Holiday number two, end of the month, saw a hive of activity, as this was the annual Gymkhana in one of their fields, which Granda kindly allowed St George's Church to use to host the event. This was a massive event for their very small village and brought the whole community together, with everyone having their own roles. Now as kids, Jane and Thomas just thought this happened by magic and it wasn't until they were useful to help put up car parking signs, build show jumps or help erect tents, that they realised how much work was actually involved.

Jane supposed this was a huge learning curve and helped her to understand the process of planning and organising a team, which stood her in good stead in later life. As a child, you really don't see the life lessons that you are learning at the time, and the benefits of what the older generation pass down to you. This is where Jane started to think now about what she is actually teaching her kids and how she can make their life an easier ride. Life is short, and we need to make each day count.

The run up to Gymkhana day was always hectic, as this usually coincided with jobs on the farm. Farmers are great multi taskers though and invariably there were last minute catastrophes that need to be sorted, but the day was always a success. Just like farming though, it was weather dependant on the day, as no one likes to wander round stalls in the pouring rain.

Grandma and Mum were always busy baking in the run up and anything that wasn't good enough for the industrial tent, would go to the ladies to serve with a cup of tea. Jane loved baking with Grandma, especially as she used to get to lick out the mixing bowl and always useful for climbing up the shelves in the pantry to reach some special ingredient required.

Day of Gymkhana was always met with excitement. Dad would be up at silly o'clock to start the show jumping, which would run all day. Chris, at the Post Office, was in charge of the gate. Granda was the Lord of the Manor, making sure everyone was having a grand day, alongside his side kick Uncle Birdus, who were invariably found in the beer tent, with a whiskey in their hands.

Armed with a pocket full of 10 pence pieces, Jane and Thomas were allowed to have a wander around on their own, under the premise that we went nowhere near the horses.

“Shall we have a go at trying to win a goldfish?” Thomas asked “Well we can try,” Jane said “although I’m not sure how happy Mum will be if we win.”

“It’ll be fine, Grandma has that big bowl in the dining room, we can use to keep it in if we win and we’ll tell Mum we’ll look after it.”

Off we wandered to the goldfish stand and – bingo, no surprises here, Thomas got two balls into the plastic cups. Goldfish in a plastic bag and a pot of fish food, Jane and Thomas walked back to the tea tent, where Grandma and Mum were helping to serve teas.

Jane could see Grandma from the entrance, hand up to her face and shaking her head, Mum was nowhere to be seen. All the old biddies from the village were like “Eeee Thomas well done you…” , “Oh there’s two in there, you must be good…”, “Wait till your Mum sees them, she’ll be so proud..”

Wait till Mum sees them was exactly what Jane was thinking, but thankfully the day was going well and Mum was extremely busy and just said “Well done, we’ll sort a bowl later” Jane was shocked, but then Mums are renowned for being shocked at the more mundane things in life, and not what you are actually concerned about.

With the day drawing to a close, they all gathered round the show jumping ring, to watch the fancy dress. A highlight of the day as this often involved some of Jane and Thomas’ friends from the village on their ponies. This was a highly sort after trophy and people went to great lengths dressing up, not just themselves, but also the ponies. Granda was always the judge and always had a tough job at picking out a winner, but there was always a prize for everyone, with sweets donated from Wormald's shop (the other shop in the village), a mix and match paper bag of goodness.

"There you go, you two," said Granda, handing us both a bag. "Plenty left for you two stars, I hear you've been winning goldfish."

Thomas was quick to reply, "Yes we thought we could use that bowl in your dining room for now?"

"Check with Grandma, but I'm sure that will be fine" said Granda, as he headed back to the beer tent.

There was a lot of tidying up to do, so Grandma, Mum, Jane and Thomas headed home. A long day for little legs, even if they were fuelled by sugar from our sweets. Jane was sure that there was a lot of tidying to do, but they didn't often see Dad and Granda until the following day. Maybe the beer tent took a lot of taking down, or maybe they headed to the club to celebrate another successful fundraiser for the church.

Chapter 4

'Start to dream big, think beyond possibilities. Our power is in the now'

-Kim Calvert

"How was school today?" asked Dad, as Jane and Thomas sat down at the kitchen table to their tea.

"Usual" said Thomas "nowt special, although I think I'm liking middle school better than first school"

"Well, that's good," said Dad "What are you enjoying the best?"

"I like the sports, there's much more choice and we're learning to play tennis properly, not just bashing a ball up against a wall," This made everyone laugh.

"What about the work though?" asked Dad, with a smile on his face.

"Well, that's ok, but the sports and making new friends is the best bit" Thomas smiled back.

"What about you Jane, you still enjoying it?" Dad asked, winking at Jane across the table "Oh yes, I love it, not long left till the next holidays though. And my final year starting in September, can't believe it, but I'll be able to keep an eye on Thomas."

Jane loved and hated school in equal amounts, first school was fine, as life was easy and carefree. But as you grow up, you start to get all the added complications of friendship groups, being split from your friends, when moving to a bigger school, and Jane lacked in confidence. Jane's friends from first school were much more outgoing than her and soon made new friends, leaving Jane on the peripheral of a group. Jane found this tough at the time, but looking back, this probably made her the strong person that she is today.

Middle School was a huge step for Jane, it was almost like starting a whole new life. Going from a class of friends of varying ages, to a year group of one hundred, split into three classes, was massive. Jane remembers sitting on the first day in Middle School, at her desk and only knowing one other person in the classroom, not a great feeling. Although Jane took each day in her stride, and to be honest, she probably daydreamed quite a lot. Looking out of the window into the countryside and constantly thinking about what Dad was busy with at home.

Jane's first three years there went over without too much drama. There were occasions when Jane was very alone, but this helped her grow as a person, enjoying her own company and focusing on her end goal, which was to get through school and make her parents proud. Jane found she was actually good at sports and enjoyed all the sports that were on offer. This probably had something to do with the lovely Mrs Robson, who was an amazing PE teacher. Jane loved spending time with her, and to be honest, she helped Jane more than she realised at the time.

Jane was keen to be involved in all sports, which made her a good all-rounder, but her main love was running, and in particular cross country, as Jane could take in the scenery as she went.

Jane's highlight at Middle School was being made Rounders captain, with her team winning for the first time in the school's history.

Jane felt like Thomas, when he was running around and chanting with Granda's cup, it was an amazing feeling, especially as Jane was picked to captain the team, above all the usual suspects.

Jane was a team player, and also excelled in Tennis and Athletics. The love of exercise and the outdoors is still evident today, as Jane loves the feeling of being at one with nature.

The weekends seemed to fly over, there was always something to do on the farm. The sheep and lambs were brought in to check on a regular basis, this gave Jane and Thomas a chance to see Menace and Blackie, who, as Dad put it, were the bain of his life, always following him around and going in the totally wrong direction. Jess, Dad's special collie, was great, but she was at a loss with these two. Jess had been Jane's special guard dog when she was in her pram outside the house, no one could get near. Jane had spent hours playing with Jess and a hosepipe, with them both ending up soaked through, hours of endless fun! Jane and Thomas were always strategically placed in a gateway, or on the yard, to turn sheep in the right direction. The sheep had to have their feet checked and, once the weather got warmer, their thick fleeces needed to be clipped off.

Sunday lunch at Gran and Granda Ben's (Dad's parents) was amazing, no one made Yorkshire puddings like Gran, or was it Auntie Gertie who made them, who knows. There was always a house full at Colepike and never a shortage of food. They too were farmers, so there was no escaping it, once lunch was over, there was usually a job for us all to help with.

"Many hands make light work" was one of Granda Ben's favourite sayings.

Lunch was 12 noon on the dot, not a minute before and not a minute after. You could actually set your clock by the mealtimes at Colepike, Granda Ben was always looking at his pocket watch around 4pm, even after a hearty Sunday lunch. Tea and cake at 4pm, then home, so Gran and Granda Ben could head off to Chapel.

Grandma would, more than likely, have all the jobs done when Jane and Thomas got home, this included milking the two goats Bangers and Mash. Thomas drank the milk to help his eczema and asthma. There was no mobile phones in those days, so they'd often hear "looks like the goats and jobs have been done, we could have stayed away a bit longer if we'd known" but you could never be sure.

"You've gone off in a daydream there Jane" said Mum.

"Ah yes, just thinking about what's next to do at home" Jane couldn't explain that things weren't great at school.

"Oh, we need to watch the weather forecast, do you think we've missed it?" said Dad

"Think we'll catch it, I'll go pop the TV on, what you planning next week Dad?" Jane asked knowingly, as they were getting round to hay time on the farm.

"We'll see what the forecast says." added Dad.

Hay making was quite a thing when Jane and Thomas were younger, as they didn't have the huge machinery that is now available to farmers. This meant that they needed a good few days of warm sunny weather to make good hay. The grass would be cut and left to dry out, so they had to have a good window of a few dry days to get it right.

"Looks promising, I think I'll pop out and get the mower on the tractor ready, to make a start in the morning." said Dad.

This was the start of the busy time, as once hay time was over, things quickly move into harvest and then getting the crops back in the ground for the following year. Jane also knew this was the start of not seeing Dad on such a regular basis again. She'd kind of got used to him being around and having tea with them after lambing time. Jane was getting older though and knew she was able to help more, and spend time with him outside, without getting in the way.

Hay time on the farm growing up was a tough time for Jane, as she suffers from hayfever, but that didn't stop her helping out though. Jane was often found stacking bales, with her eyes watering and continuously sneezing. Jane and Thomas loved watching the baler pop out the square bales as they called them, but actually they were more rectangle shaped. They used to feed the sheep, cows and of course, Dad's horses during the winter months, so it had to be right. It was a community feel during hay time, as Dad and Granda asked the men from the village to help stack the bales in the field onto a trailer and then once they were led back to the farm, they were stacked into the shed to keep them dry. The men who helped, all lived in the village, and most had worked in the coal mine, which was on the farm and were well used to manual work. The elevator was used to send the bales to the top of the stack in the shed, but this was extremely temperamental and Granda's maintenance skills were often called on.

Once the hay was safely gathered in, the sheep needed to be clipped (adult sheep only), this was always a fun few days, but once again, weather dependant, as the wool has to be dry to get it off the sheep.

"You two happy to help Albert (one of the local men who helped out) wrap fleeces today?" shouted Dad up the stairs. "Looks like a good day for it".

Jane rolled over in bed, thinking that all she wanted to do was lie there, she pulled herself together and grabbed her oldest jeans and a raggy t-shirt. No use wearing anything good, as the lanolin from the wool left everything greasy, but it was great for hands! Jane bombed downstairs, grabbed a quick glass of milk and out the door, closely followed by Thomas.

Dad had already set off to gather the sheep. "Be good to see Menace and Blackie," said Thomas

"Yes it will, I can't believe they have lambs of their own this year again, we have our own little flock of sheep!" Jane added.

"I still can't believe Dad has let us keep them for as long, as they are a total pain." he laughed.

Jane and Thomas were continually reminded of the pain in the bum the two sheep were, but Dad had been keen for them to have an interest, and selling the lambs from their two original pet lambs, helped them to understand the process of raising the lambs and selling them. Neither Jane nor Thomas found this easy to understand, until they had their own lambs that were sent to the local auction mart to sell for meat.

Jane and Thomas knew exactly where they needed to stand when Dad was bringing sheep into the yard to work with. At their stations ready and waiting as always, taking in the smell of the honeysuckle growing on the side of the cottage. The sheep were soon in the yard, Blackie and Menace slowed down on their way past, but Jane and Thomas didn't speak. They ran the flock through the stone buildings, and shed the lambs off the ewes and let them back to the field to graze, while their mums had a haircut. The blearing was unreal, but the lambs soon calmed down and lay down next to the gate in the field, waiting expectantly for their mums to return.

The scene was set and the clipping machines were soon whirring away, removing the heavy wool coats of the ewes. You can almost see the relief on their faces, especially if it is a warm day. It is harder than it looks clipping a ewe, as they don't always sit still, and can wriggle and kick, thus leaving you with lots of cuts and bruises. Jane still says the hardest part is wrapping the fleeces and packing the wool into bags, wrapping outside in the heat, on a black plastic sheet, is no fun in the heat of the day. It's a good workout though.

"Grubs up" shouted Mum and Grandma, over the whirring of the clipping machines.

Ham sandwiches, and jam sandwiches for Thomas, with a huge urn of tea. The urn was originally used to deliver milk to people when they had dairy cows. It is hard to describe, but the urn looked like a big biscuit tin, with a handle and lid. Albert and his brother Ronnie had lived in the village all their lives and loved coming to help out. It was great to hear some of their stories from the coal mining days, whilst they all sat and had lunch in the shade. Lunch didn't last long, as Dad and Geoff didn't want to sit too long, as they soon cooled down and then their whole body would start to ache, especially their backs. Dad and Geoff also clipped for other people, to get a bit of extra cash.

Chapter 5

"Smell the sea and feel the sky. Let your soul and spirit fly."

-Van Morrison

School was school, and Jane will always have good, and bad memories, both making her the strong person that she is today. If Jane was to be totally honest, she lived for the weekends, and helping out at nights, after school, and of course, the school holidays. Friends always told her how lucky she was to grow up on a farm and at the time, you don't fully appreciate the life lessons that you are learning and how this can help you out in later life; you never realise. Jane almost felt like she was missing out on the fun side of life, being in a village surrounded by friends, playing out every night, but she knew she was growing for the future person.

Jane and Thomas had great times when the nights got lighter and, as they got older, friends used to come and spend time on the farm. Jane couldn't speak for them all, but she was sure that they too learnt some life lessons. How they are all still here today is beyond Jane, as they were often found climbing on the roof tops of buildings, during a game of hide and seek;~~,~~ or up the conker tree in the pasture;~~,~~ on top of the hay stack in the shed and sometimes hiding in the corn byre, where Dad stored the feed, sometimes even up on the 3rd floor, after climbing up the rickety ladders. Happy kids, with not a care in the world. Mum's caramel shortbread was always a big hit when friends visited.

Growing up on a farm can have its disadvantages too, as everyone is always too busy to do this, or too busy to do that. Mum was always there as Jane and Thomas's taxi to take and collect us from school, and all the after school clubs, we found ourselves at.

Jane and Thomas were lucky as children and always had a family holiday, usually first two weeks of the school holidays, in July. Jane's first recollection of being on holiday is to Scarborough, where the family stayed in a flat, with a yellow door, and a short walk from the beach.. Jane and Thomas had great fun playing in the sand and enjoyed having Dad's full attention, for the whole two weeks of the holiday, they built sandcastles, dug , dabbled and had the occasional donkey ride. This was a novelty, and as they grew older, they realised this was a precious time, as Dad had no distractions. Although he did like to have a drive around to see what other farmers were doing, just in case he was getting behind while he was away. They often visited the local Livestock Auction Mart, just to see what prices the local farmers were getting for their produce.

As Jane and Thomas got older, they did venture further field for holidays, with many weeks spent on the South coast, in Cornwall and Devon. What a drive that was - but always a fun time when they got there, often stuck in traffic jams on Bodmen Moor. It always made Jane laugh that the locals came along through the traffic, selling ice creams.

"Looks like a canny day for the beach," said Dad.

"Yes let's go, I'll get my spade" said Thomas.

It was always like loading up for a full adventure, buckets, spades, windshield (just in case), a picnic and the kitchen sink! Well, it would've been included, had they had a one to transport.

A short drive to the beach.

"Everyone grab something to carry" shouted Mum, too late, as Thomas had grabbed his spade and was off.

"I'll catch him up," Jane said, grabbing the blue and orange cool box.

"I'm digging here" said Thomas.

"Yep, that looks like a good spot" Jane replied, putting the cool box down and sitting on it. She took off her shoes and socks, and felt the sand on her feet - so relaxing.

"You two certainly know when to dash off," heaved Dad, as he joined us, carrying the stripy wood deck chairs and windshield, closely followed by Mum, with the spare bags of clothes.

"We need a big stone to knock the poles in for the windshield," said Dad.

Off Jane went on the look out. It was great to walk on the sand, the feeling of the dry sand running through your toes and finding the connection with the earth.

"This do?" Jane asked, holding up a canny rock that she had found.

"Perfect" said Dad. windshield up and deck chairs positioned, we were set for the day.

"Suncream kids." said Mum

"Argh Mam" replied Thomas, never one to volunteer to the suncream, think it's a boy thing.

All creamed up, Thomas continued to dig, Jane thought he wanted to dig to Australia!

They all had a wander to the sea, to wash off the sand from building and digging, then they all sat down for their well-deserved picnic lunch.

"Fancy meeting you here," came a voice from behind the windshield.

"Ha, how did you know we were here?" Jane asked. "What a surprise!"

It was Auntie Margaret and Uncle Peter, Julie and Jamie "Well we just happened to be nearby and were sure we saw you from the car park," said Auntie Margaret.

Jane certainly didn't believe that. "Really?" Jane asked.

"No, we are holidaying down here too and thought you might like some company, Julie and Jamie thought it would be a fun afternoon too." said Auntie Margaret.

Well, that made their day, Julie is the same age as Jane, and Jamie a little younger than Thomas. So the scene was set, the grown-ups were happy and all the children were happy too.

They spent the whole day at the beach and enjoyed building sandcastles, playing rounders and cricket and, of course, the odd dip in the sea.

As the day went by, the wind picked up "Lucky we set the windshield up," said Dad "Maybe the kite would fly now?" he questioned. Jane for one didn't believe he could get it flying, but as she learnt over the years, he is determined. Maybe that's where Jane gets it from.

Jamie was keen to see it fly before they headed away, so with kite assembled and Thomas in charge of the string handles - off they went.

Obviously, there was no phones to video in those days and they didn't have the Super 8 movie camera to hand, but Jane so wished she could have recorded this. Dad set off along the beach at a hundred miles an hour, kite in hand and was too busy shouting "Get ready Thomas, get ready, Thomas, NOW" as he threw the kite in the air. Thomas was actually good at flying it, Jamie was celebrating, and all was good, but it wasn't too last. Down it came. "Right Dad again, I've got it this time." shouted Thomas.

Thankfully there wasn't many people left on the beach, as Dad took off on his next run, just as he launched the kite and was about to celebrate, his flip flops, not Dad's favourite footwear, decided to snap and he tripped over a stone, landing in a heap in the sand, all in slow motion to us sitting on the deck chairs. None of them were in any fit state to ask how he was, poor Dad, they were all totally creased laughing.

"Aye don't worry about me," said Dad "Have a good laugh at my expense." As he stood up and brushed himself down.

"It was kinda hilarious though" Jane cheekily commented, knowing she probably wouldn't have if Auntie Margaret had not been there.

"No more kite for me today." said Dad.

"You ok Dad?" asked Thomas, as him and Jamie came running over.

"Yes I'm fine Thomas, thanks for asking. These lot just think it's hilarious!"

Pride bruised and, no doubt a bit tender, they all packed up for the day and headed for fish and chips, a holiday treat, as Mum usually cooked in the holiday home. A fab day was had by all, a comment that would be used in future, on a regular basis.

Dad got the last laugh though the following day. Having spent most of the day building sandcastles with Jamie, Thomas had managed to burn his heals, the suncream obviously missed that bit.

"I can't go anywhere today!" explained Thomas , with a pained look on his face.

"I'm not exactly fit today either," replied Dad.

"I know, you can wear a pair of my socks, so the sun doesn't get to your heels again" Jane suggested.

"Not likely," said Thomas. But he was totally outnumbered, as they had already planned their day.

"I don't want to miss out on the Monkey Sanctuary though, so I suppose I'll have too" Thomas said in a very, very disappointed voice.

"Bonus will be Dad might have to carry you if your feet get really sore" Jane winked.

And off they all went, Thomas dressed in Jane's lovely white ankle socks. What a picture! They did have a wonderful day, watching the monkeys, Thomas felt completely at home.

It's amazing to think, it's where humans all came from, in some shape or form, as evolution happens and at a young age, actually hard to accept.

On their way back to the holiday house, they called at a gnome garden, one of Mum's findings, literally someone's house, with a gnome trail around the garden. Jane and Thomas arrived all excited about gnomes and fairies, they were given a felt gnome hat to wear. There was no way Dad doing this, so they all had a good laugh at his expense again.

Happy days, there are many stories of holidays to tell that Jane could go on for hours. The moral of this is that family time is precious and, no matter how short a time, memories will be made that will last a lifetime and entertain future generations, giving them an insight into a past life. It also teaches us, as grown-ups, that we need to make our own family memories too.

The drive home was always a nightmare, but thankfully no traffic jams. Although it often involved a detour as a wrong turn was taken, Mum wasn't the best map reader in the world, no google maps, or sat nav in those days!

Once home and fully recharged, life on the farm continued. The daily rituals of sheep work and nurturing the crops ready for harvest continued.

Coffee time at the Big House following a holiday, be it Jane and Thomas', or Grandma and Granda', were always filled with laughter and the full rundown of what had happened, while either party had been away. There was always a tale of woe of some description. Things didn't always run smoothly on the farm, there are always trials and tribulations. Dad and Granda occasionally had a major fall out over something or other, and it wasn't the easiest of times for any of them. And the usual "Don't you two dare go along there today" from Mum.

These were usually resolved by Mum having a chat with Grandma, and things would soon return to normal, with Jane and Thomas being allowed back along the yard to visit. It's a generation thing and a working with an in-law, rather than family. Not an easy situation for anyone to be in, but it always worked out in the end. Dad is very like Jane in that respect and is very patient, but when his patience is tested to the limit, he snaps and you make a sharp exit.

Grandma and Granda had some amazing holidays, and they were always great at sharing their experiences. They loved to cruise and due to Grandma being unable to fly, they travelled by train from Newcastle to Southampton, to board the Oriana, to set sail on their travels. Jane would go with Dad to drop them off at the station, this one day and they were chatting away in the car on route to Newcastle Central station, when all of a sudden Granda exclaims "I've forgotten my bloody teeth!!"

Grandma and Jane tried all ways not to burst out laughing, but to no avail.

"Aye well it's alright for you lot, with your own teeth" Granda replied.

Dad quickly turned the car around and the teeth were duly retrieved from the Big House. Granda, his teeth and Grandma were safely delivered to the station, Dad and Jane helped them onto the train, with their luggage and waited to wave them off on their travels. Dad and Jane had a good laugh on the way home about the teeth situation, Granda never wore his teeth regularly and carried them round in the pocket of his checky shirt, only putting them in if someone visited, so it was no wonder they were forgotten.

Three weeks past and not going to lie, family life was always that little bit more relaxed, when they weren't at home.

“Who’s coming to collect Grandma and Granda with me today?” asked Mum.

“Think I’m out helping Dad,” said Thomas “but we’ll be back for the coffee catch up.”

“I’ll come” said Jane, she loved the first chatter, in the car, on the way home.

“Let’s go then.” said Mum.

Car parked up in Newcastle Station, Mum and Jane headed to the platform. They didn’t have to wait long before the train pulled in. They could see Grandma and Granda waving, as the train drew to a stop, at the platform. Bags loaded onto a trolley, they noticed Granda wasn’t walking too great.

“You ok Dad?” asked Mum

“That’s a whole story in itself,” he replied, “I’ll fill you in in the car.”

Grandma winked at Jane, with a smile on her face, what story would they get - obviously something had happened.

As Mum and Jane loaded the car and left central station, the stories began. The cruise around the Caribbean had been amazing, with stop offs at various islands. Then there had been a short stop at the Canary Islands, on the way home.

“This is where the story gets interesting…” said Grandma

“Please don’t laugh” said Granda

“Oh, what could possibly have gone wrong?” Jane asked.

“Well in Lanzarote, often nicknamed the windy island, it was a glorious day, so Granda and me decided to have a wander onto the beach, he even put his shorts on!”

Grandma continued “We paddled in the warm sea and even chilled on the deckchairs for a short while, all was good, as we embarked back onto the P&O cruise ship. It wasn’t until we were getting ready for the Captain’s dinner that Granda realised there was something wrong, his legs were starting to blister, not very pretty, hence his walking isn't great"

She leant over to Jane and whispered in her ear "He's actually wearing a pair of my tights!"

Well Jane remembers not being able to hold in her giggle, now whilst Granda was all for a joke, he wasn't the best when the joke was on him.

"It's nothing to laugh about, it is not very comfortable you know"

And until Jane went abroad in later life, she didn't realise how painful sunburn can be.

Mum and Jane got Grandma and Granda home, and the kettle on in the big house, waiting for Dad and Thomas to get in, for the holiday debrief.

Chapter 6

'Don't judge each day by the harvest you reap, but by the seeds you plant. Harvest the good and forget the rest'

-Brian Cassidy

Holidays well and truly behind the family, the farm work started in earnest, with harvest. This is where the crops that were planted in October of the previous year, get combined, with the combine harvester, nicknamed the yellow peril. This is a busy time, as with most jobs on the farm, it is also weather dependant, as the crop has to be dry, this is explained in more detail below.

"Forecast is looking good for this week" explained Dad on Sunday night, after watching the farming weather forecast.

"Hopefully we'll get some of it done before we have to go back to school." said Thomas.

"Yes, be good if we can. Then you can help stack the straw bales," Dad said hopefully.

Thankfully the straw bales were a lot easier for Jane and Thomas' little bodies to roll around, to help get them to the stack, much lighter than hay bales.

"Early beds then, because I'm straight onto the yellow peril to start combining in the morning. I'll give Derek a ring, to see if he's free to help Granda lead from over the railway."

Dad was keen for Jane and Thomas to be bright and breezy in the morning, as they were useful opening and closing gates, and also stacking the straw, if everything went to plan.

"I take it that you'll need me to man the railway gates?" asked Mum.

"Yes, or we can ask Flo if she's happy to sit on her deckchair. I'll pop down and put the signs on the road now, so people know not to park on the side of the road, otherwise the yellow peril will never get down" Dad was on a roll.

Jane and Thomas looked at each other and both announced at the same time "Think I'll head to bed now" and made a sharp exit, before they got another job.

Surprisingly, the sun shone brightly through the curtains the next morning, not that it was ever in doubt, as it looked like a very settled period of weather, action stations all round.

For years as littlies, Jane and Thomas had watched Dad combining, this was the first time they had actually felt helpful.

"Do you think Dad will let me sit up top on the yellow peril with him?" exclaimed Thomas, as he came flying into the kitchen.

"We'll have to wait and see, it gets kinda dusty up there, you've seen the state Dad comes in after a day up there. He looks like he's been down the pit." said Mum.

"Eh what do you mean?" asked Thomas.

"Well, the dust settles on Dad's face, while he's combining, just like when Albert and Ronnie used to work in the coal mine, which they called the pit, hence Dad looks like he's been down the pit" explained Mum.

"Ah that makes sense. So would I look like I'd been down the pit too?" asked Thomas.

"No, if you go up onto yellow peril, we'll try and find you a mask, or tie a damp hankie around your face, then you can look like a cowboy" Mum giggled

"But we'll wait and see how things go, you know how temperamental the old girl is. Dad is just busy greasing her up, while the dew evaporates, if you want to go help with that?"

Thomas was straight out the door, just a quick glass of his Bangers and Mash goat's milk, the only part of his daily ritual that he managed to keep.

“No idea why I suggested that! He’ll be up to the eyes before he even sees the combine moving. Do you mind helping me make some caramel shortbread and scones for the field teas, I am hoping they will need this week?” asked Mum

“Yes, that’s fine,” Jane replied.

Jane loved spending time with Mum, or Grandma, at the kitchen bench, learning the skills of baking. Although her attempts were never the best, but as they say - practise makes perfect - and it certainly helped Jane run her home in later life. There is something quite soothing about rubbing lard and flour together for scones, it’s almost like a massage for your hands.

“What about rock buns Mum, they always go down a treat,”

“Oh yes that's a good idea. Can you check that we have all the ingredients?” so off Jane toddled with the recipe, one of Gran’s old recipes, written on a scrap of paper, usually tucked in the recipe note book. Jane’s little hands could not carry everything together, so numerous trips later she delivered the ingredients. Then Mum and Jane cracked on to make the rock buns.

“Bring, bring bring” went the green house phone, Mum wiped her hands on her pinny “bring bring” and made a dash for the telephone.

“That was Grandma checking that we had plenty stuff for teas. She’s been on baking too, so we can freeze some of this, for your packed lunches.”

“Cool,” Jane replied “Do we need to do anything else” she asked.

“No, I think we are ready for action. Just keep your fingers and toes crossed that the Yellow Peril starts and keeps going!” said Mum.

Now, when Jane was young, she knew she could cross her fingers, but always wondered how on earth do you cross your toes? As Jane learnt as she grew up, there are numerous sayings, that as kids, they'd pick up and carry on into their lives, and pass down to their own children. Jane was sure there will be more as the story unfolds.

Dad and Thomas arrived back at the house, as Mum had said previously, Thomas was up to the eyes (There's another one of those sayings).

"Think you need the Swarfega to get the oil and grease off those hands, before you have a snack and a drink." exclaimed Mum.

"Yeah, but it was cool. I got to crawl under the combine to make sure Dad had got everything greased" said Thomas, proud as punch.

"Yes I can see that" said Mum, raising her eye brows at Dad.

"Are we a go?"

"Most certainly. I've had an expert helper this morning and if all goes well, he can have a sit up top, when he brings the lunch stop bait down" said Dad.

"Whoop whoop" shouted Thomas as he punched the air.

Quick cuppa and Dad was straight back out. It was quite a short journey over the railway, to the first field that Dad wanted to cut. Mum knew that Jane and Thomas would want to go down, as Jimmy Mouse and his friends lived down there, so once we heard the combine start up, they headed down. The road down to the river is quite narrow and, hopefully, after the sign was put out last night, no cars would've parked, but there was usually always one. A combine is slow moving, so Thomas, Mr Grease Lightning, flew down the road, with Jane and Mum hot on his tail!

"Don't forget to stop at the railway" Mum huffed.

"It's ok, I know I'm just checking that there's no cars." Thomas shouted back.

They made it to the railway and thankfully, the fishermen had all taken heed of Dad's make shift sign and parked in the turning space. So the yellow peril would make it straight down and over the railway, ready for action. Whilst combining is exciting to watch, Jane and Thomas soon lost interest, so with Mum, they walked along to the clearing, down to the river to throw in some stones. Mum was really good at skimming the stones, so they bounced across the water. The weather had been good with not much rain, so there were plenty stones to climb on and jump from one to another.

Jane and Thomas managed to stay dry and, as they walked back up, had a quick look to see if Jimmy mouse was home, no luck. They'd have to tell Granda later, he must be away on his holidays now.

They all waved at Dad on the way past, and headed back home, to get the lunch bait ready.

"When we come back down with the lunch, I'm sure Dad will let you have a sit up top, or it may be better to wait until teatime, once they've made a bit of headway" Mum said to Thomas.

"Excellent! Happy either way, as long as I get a go" he replied.

Mum went straight into the house, to start packing the sandwiches.

"Anyone home?" came a voice from the door, it was Grandma.

"Mum is just busy getting sandwiches ready for lunchtime."

"Oh, I'll give her a hand, I've got the cakes sorted for tea." said Grandma.

"And the tea urn?" Jane asked

"Oh yes," replied Grandma "The guys love their tea from the tea urn."

They hadn't even had lunch and Grandma was talking about tea. She was in her element, feeding the masses and to be fair, Jane loved a field tea. As a little person, it was fun running through the straw that the combine put out the back, once it had harvested the grain, although Dad and Granda were always shouting at us, as it made the baling job harder, if the straw was spread all over.

They watched from the living room window, as the yellow peril went slowly backwards and forwards, along the field, harvesting the crop, wheat - which has all sorts of uses, depending on the quality. Once the combine tank was full of wheat, it had to be emptied into a trailer. That was Derek's job.

"Quick Jane, they're emptying!" shouted Thomas.

Jane and Thomas loved to watch the tractor and trailer pull alongside, to empty, as the combine kept rolling. Jane secretly thought they were waiting for the disaster of Derek driving too fast, or too slow, and the wheat shooting off the side, but it was a smooth transfer and Derek was soon heading back up to the farm, to tip the trailer load of wheat into the hemmel, for storage until it was decided where it was to go to next.

So, it was a quick shift to the kitchen window to see Derek reversing the trailer round to empty.

"You two stay in here," shouted Mum "Derek doesn't need any more distractions. It's a difficult reverse round there."

Dutifully, Jane and Thomas stood on the kitchen bench. Derek gave them a wave and they both giggled, and waved back.

"We'll be doing that one day." said Thomas.

The novelty of watching the yellow peril and the tractor soon wore off, as neither Jane nor Thomas felt very useful. The excitement increased after lunch, Grandma had delivered the lunchtime feed, so when Mum suggested getting the paddling pool out, it was cheers all round, what could possibly go wrong? Watched over by a very excited Penny, Jane and Thomas played in the garden, occasionally popping their heads over the gate to see the tractor tipping, or standing checking Dad was still going backwards and forwards. It was inevitable really that the three of them ended up in the paddling pool, pure relief on the face of Penny to get cooled down. Fun and laughter was to be heard all around.

"Time to get dried off and dressed, so we can take the tea down, Grandma is on her way along with the tea." said Mum from the front door.

Jane and Thomas raced up the steps and into the house, closely followed by a very wet Penny.

"Argh man," exclaimed Mum "the dog is soaked!" as Penny shook herself dry at the kitchen steps, leaving a trail of wet footprints through the dining room and kitchen.

The four of them - Mum, Grandma, Jane and Thomas, laden with the baskets and the tea urn, headed out on the short walk to the riverside field. Albert, Ronnie and Peter were also there, as Peter had started baling the straw, but there was still plenty loose straw for us to run around in. We even helped roll some bales across to Ronnie and Albert, so they could stack them into the 18's (18 bales) to be picked up by the carrier, on the back of the tractor, to lead them all home. Penny loved jumping in and out with them too, lots of nice smells. The chat at teatime was always a great chance to catch up on the gossip in the village, and hear stories of the coal mine, and how things used to look. As littlies, they didn't pay much attention, but as they we grew, they found it more and more interesting, better than reading a book.

Now, this is a snapshot of one day harvesting, harvesting even for the family on the small scale, was a lot longer, than one day with harvest, sometimes being drawn out over a period of weeks, or even months, depending on the weather.

Back to the here and now............ a bonus bit

'It is what it is! And it will be what it is'

-Brian Cassidy

"This has been hard, what is normal life, it seems like a lifetime ago." The end of my first bit of writing about me, and starting a snapshot into my early life growing up on a farm. I have been given this opportunity to share a small part of my story. I have always dreamt of writing a book, in my head, it would have been a children's book, but with the life changing traumas that my family and I have gone through during the past year and well really nearing 2 years, I wanted to delve deep into my inner self, test my memory and remember the experiences of growing up.

February 2023 gives you a sneak peek into what might follow, if I decide to write more. That is entirely up to you, my reader. Let me know your thoughts, details at the end of the bonus read, and at the end of chapter 12.

I am sat in our apartment overlooking Loch Tay, with the snow-capped mountain of Ben Lawers as a back drop. Totally off camber to the story that I am currently telling.

I feel inspired to write, so here you have a little bonus. I am here at the Scottish Winter Championships to support my daughter, Charlotte, in her swimming and also to take part myself. The outdoor swimming community is a fantastic family to be part of, and during these past few months they have helped me enormously. The buzz you get from a cold dip is unreal, and the endorphins that are released, keep you going for hours. Charlotte started swimming outdoors in 2019 and hasn't looked back.

I, like many of you reading, was one of the "you'll never get me in there" group, until one day, after driving Charlotte to our lifeguarded venue, on a cool Sunny Saturday. I was stood on the side of the lake, watching her swim and my mind drifted back to all the swimming lessons that I'd had as a child. The swimming galas that I'd swam in and the fun I'd had on family holidays. I'm a swimmer at heart, I thought to myself. What am I doing on the side watching, I'm driving Charlotte here and I might as well be in there with her. It was like a light bulb moment. Once Charlotte was finished, I approached her coach and got myself booked in for a 'one to one' session introduction to cold water swimming. I've never looked back.

If I ever feel down with life, and need a reset or pick me up, a cool dip soon does the job. I've also been found to travel miles, to meet up with like-minded ladies, to go for a dip. I have made some amazing new friends, who get the buzz and the community spirit. Hence, I find myself two years down the line, competing at the Scottish Winter Championships, 50m freestyle not my best swim in the world, but I did it.

Unfortunately, due to unforeseen circumstances, the event had to be cancelled on the Saturday lunchtime. It was a bit of a downer, but everyone understood the reasons and we still had our presentations to look forward too. Any other event may have ended in a lot of arguing and unhappy people, but not today. As I look out of the window, the sun starts to set behind the mountains, how could anyone be angry with a view like that. It just goes to show how a community of like-minded people can make the best of something. Plans were quickly in place for a fun afternoon in hot tubs, and a social evening in the pub on site, followed by an after party. All things happen for a reason and there is always an outcome worth having. Gratitude for all the hard work that the organisers put in and pure understanding.

It has been the most amazing space to spend time with Charlotte, and start creating our new memories.

It means that I've been given the chance to write to you, my reader, with a snippet of what might follow in future stories. Let me know your thoughts, by contacting me via:

via email: janeaanderson1@gmail.com

Facebook: Jane Anderson

Instagram: jane_a_anderson

LinkedIn: Jane Anderson

Chapter 7

'Just because you think it doesn't mean it's true. Whatever you think today creates tomorrow'

-Ciaran Deaney

The days ticked by, Dad spending long hours, driving the yellow peril to get the crops in, while the weather was dry, so family dinner and tea trips were their chance to catch up and get a cuddle. It is a whole team effort and once the combining of a field is finished, it is a quick check on the weather forecast, and a decision made to move onto another field to combine, or gather in the straw and get it undercover and stacked in the shed, alongside the hay. The little bales of straw were usually all stacked into 18sin the field, and left to be led to the shed, another day, as getting the crop in dry was more important.

The daily chores still needed to be done, while Dad and Granda were busy, so it was down to Mum, Grandma and their little helpers. Bangers and Mash still needed to milked twice a day, the dogs needed to be exercised, usually incorporated into a walk to the field. All the stock had to be looked at, to check they were all where they should be, and in good health. Now, harvest time requires dry weather, but this has its own consequences, as with the dry spells of weather, the family needed to keep an eye on the amount of grass for the stock and sometimes, they had to give them some of the hay, made earlier in the year, for the winter feeding. So, as farmers, they were grateful for the dry spells to get the crops in, but it has an adverse effect of the growth of the grass to feed the stock. It's like a continuous juggling act and quick decisions need to be made, and actioned.

As it was usually during the summer holidays from school, there was always an influx of Jane and Thomas' friends wanting to come and play. There's nothing more inviting than a heap of grain to race up and down, and play in. It is a strange sensation with the grain on skin and, nine times out of ten, they were caught in the act and given a dressing down by Mum.

But it also gave their friends an insight into farming life. They were always keen to cover their tracks, using the brush to sweep the trails of grain back to the heap. But they always forgot that their shoes were full, and a trail of grain followed them, from the hemmel, back to the house, like Hansel and Gretel. So, no matter how hard they denied being there, it was always obvious. The farm was Jane and Thomas' playground and, as they grew, they had to learn the risks of the different areas that they played in. To be honest, health and safety would've had a fit, but that was then, and Mum and Dad were health and safety. So, as long as Jane and Thomas looked out for each other, Mum and Dad didn't intervene too much. It's not till Jane looks back now, that she realised the potential hazard! Jane is sure that they were warned at the time, about actually drowning in a large heap of grain. This is the learning they grew up with, and it helped them in later life, to assess the risks.

Six weeks of summer holidays seems like a lifetime when you are young, and with the family's two weeks away on a family holiday, the remaining four weeks would fly by. There was the annual trip to get school uniform, with Mum and Grandma. Usually left until the last week of the holidays, just in case Jane and Thomas grew, never one for being too organised, it was a last minute dash to Prudhoe, to Appleby's, the local uniform stockist.

This wasn't Thomas's favourite pastime, he hated shopping. So, on a dank and dismal morning, nearing the end of the holidays, Mum got both Jane and Thomas up and dressed in 'easy to change' clothes, as she called it.

"Make sure you're wearing your school socks as I think that you both need new shoes" she said.

"My school socks are full of barley ands" said Thomas. This is a very annoying bit of the spike from the barley head, that is left on the grain, and is a bit like having a thistle, or spelk of wood, in your sock.

"Surely not ever single pair?" replied Mum. He was just putting off actually going.

"You two ready?" shouted Grandma, she loved a trip to the shops, and spending money on Jane and Thomas - they were well and truly spoilt, to be honest.

"If all goes well, we can get fish and chips at Ball's (chip shop, still trading), as long as we don't need to go further afield for anything that Appleby's haven't got in."

Well, that did the trick, they were soon loaded up into the car and driving along to Prudhoe. Prudhoe was a bustling high street when Jane and Thomas were little. Jane recalls Mum telling stories of the old Rio cinema and The Rex, which would later be pulled down and replace by, what is now, the CO-OP.

Now, having a blazer that would last for the full four years of Highfield Middle School, the sleeves turned up, so they could be let down when Jane grew, she only needed new shoes. Thomas needed the full uniform, as this was his first year. Jane was looking forward to having a laugh at him trying on the blazers, just as he had with her.

They all wandered up to Appleby's and in the door, the tinkle of the bell as they entered. Jane recalls the ground floor being full of clothes, all be it vague, "shoes first" suggested Mum. So, they made their way up the narrow winding staircase and sat on the wooden chairs awaiting their turn.

Grandma and Mum knew the lady serving and as always, entered into a long conversation about nothing. Jane and Thomas just looked at each other,

"Look the sun's getting out," said Thomas as they looked through the very narrow windows, across the street. "Dad will be wanting to get on with the combining, I think he's nearly finished."

The lady came to both Jane and Thomas and bent down, to measured their feet with a Clark's foot measure, no electronic version in those days. Shoes all chosen and fitted, they all headed back down to the blazers, helped along by a man, in a suit, with a tape measure hanging round his neck. Thomas was measured and started trying on blazers, Jane couldn't hold in her giggle, as Mum suggested a size up, same as Jane.

"It'll last you" Mum commented. Thomas just grimaced. All shoes and uniform bagged and paid for by Grandma, they all walked up to Ball's to get their treat of fish and chips for lunch.

"Can we stop for a 10p mix up?" asked Thomas "No I think we should get back, the chips will get cold" said mum. "I need a few bits from the Post Office" said Grandma putting her thumb up to Jane and Thomas in the back of the car "I need stamps to send the cheques off, to pay the bills and a couple of letters to go, too." We pulled up outside the Post Office and raced in, the bell dinging on the door as we went. 10p mix ups, stamps and bread were loaded back into the car and they were home in no time.

The four of them sat out at the backdoor of the house, on the deckchairs in the sunshine, eating the fish and chips out of the newspaper, yes proper newspaper! Still warm, otherwise they'd have never heard the end of it. As always, the fish and chips were amazing.

"Can either of you remember where Dad said he was starting today?" asked Mum

"Think he said up the lonnen," replied Thomas.

"Ah well, we'll have a tootal up later and see how he's getting on, we can maybe call in and see the Browns on the way." said Mum. Penny was sitting begging for any scraps, her usual pose when food was on the go. As always, she did get the odd chip that was accidently dropped.

Tummies full, Jane and Thomas chilled for a bit on the deckchairs, but like most kids, we were soon up and playing in the garden, leaving Grandma and Mum to chat. It was great to enjoy a bit of the sunshine. It was soon time for a walk up to see Dad. Up the lonnen, they went and sure enough, Phil, Irene and Michael were in the garden, working hard as always. Michael was in the shade in his pram, Jane and Thomas made a bee line for the pram.

"No kids, I've just got him off to sleep. Call on the way back and you can see him then." whispered Irene, as she intercepted them on route.

They continued along the lonnen, and found Dad and Granda finishing up the combining, and getting set to head back to get the baler.

"Get in, I'll get a ride back in the tractor, my legs are so sore from walking." exclaimed Thomas, he wasn't one for exercise.

Mum looked at Jane and said, "It's ok, we can call and have a chat with Irene, so you can see Michael" Jane smiled back.

Mum and Jane let the team head back and called the dogs in, and walked back to the bungalow to see the Brown's. They knew before they got there, that they could see Michael because they could hear the screams!

"Maybe we'll just sneak past?" said Mum.

"No, it'll be ok, Michael likes me" Jane said.

Once into the beautifully manicured garden, they wandered over to where Phil and Irene were sitting having a cuppa.

"Want one?" said Phil raising his mug.

"No, it's fine," said Mum "just a quick visit. It's back to school tomorrow, so we need to get sorted. We just called to see how the little fella was doing."

"Did you not hear him screaming? I can't keep him full." said Irene.

Michael was lifted from his pram and passed to Mum, who cradled him in her arms and then passed him to Jane for a hold. Well, that didn't last long, as he started screaming again. Mum and Jane left soon after, and headed past Jimmy mouse's friend's tree trunk and back home, to start and prepare for school, which definitely meant an early night. Thomas was full of it when he got back, Dad had let him sit on his knee and help drive the tractor.

The uniforms were laid out in our bedrooms and the briefcases, and PE kit, ready to pick up in the kitchen, all eventualities covered. Dad was on polishing our school shoes, as we headed to bed "they need to be shining for you to wear tomorrow" he said "They're new, they don't need an extra polish" Jane replied, he just winked back, polishing away with his yellow duster.

Chapter 8

'If I wanna be free, I gotta be me. You are you're only problem; you are your own solution'

-Brian Cassidy

September, the start of another school year and Jane's last at Highfield Middle. Thomas starting his journey into big school, after being at the local Mickley First school, with just under one hundred pupils, to a year group of ninety. It certainly was a big school.

Neither Jane nor Thomas were too fussed about going back to school, as Dad and Granda were still flat out on the farm, and there was plenty for Jane and Thomas to be watching. But life is all about education and systems, and at that age, you are told what you have to do. So dutifully Jane and Thomas were out of bed and dressed in their new school uniforms, and headed out to "Mum's taxi".

Dad just had time to give us a "Looking smart as carrots you two. Enjoy your first day at big school Thomas. Don't worry we'll still be busy when you get back."

Grandma was out from the Big House, to wave Jane and Thomas off too. Not sure how Mum did it, but she took us both to school throughout our school life. Although she wasn't a great morning person either, they always made it to school.

"I'm a bit nervous about this," said Thomas "Do you think I'll be in a class with my friends?"

"You'll be fine, you make friends, no bother. There will be at least one person you know in your form class." Jane told him.

"Well, I'd much rather be helping Dad at home, but I suppose it'll be worth a go for one day." Mum and Jane giggled, as they all headed up the bank, through Mickley and turned towards Prudhoe. They were soon at school and jumped out of the car, with their briefcases, and headed into school.

Meanwhile back on the farm, Dad was still harvesting some fields, whilst Granda was busy ploughing the fields that had already been harvested, baled and cleared. The cycle of replanting the fields, for next year's crops, was starting again, with some fields left until the early spring of the following year. As said previously, there is no real quiet time on the farm and it is all very weather dependant.

There is also the added pressure of selling the lambs that would soon be ready for market, Dad liked to leave this job for a weekend, so that Jane and Thomas could help get them in from the field, and then sort into batches for the Auction Mart. Jane and Thomas loved being involved and to be honest, it helped get Jane through her school days, being able to help on the farm. Mum was great and took Jane and Thomas to the after school clubs that they were involved in, but the joy of being close to nature, and animals, will always be with them.

Jane is forever grateful that she was born into a farming family and taught by three generations about how to grow up to nurture and respect nature, and the environment that we live in. Dad's Grandparents were still farming when we were little, and to hear some of the proper olden day stories was awesome. Life has moved so quickly, in such a short space of time, it's hard to imagine where we will be in another 50 years.

On this note, Jane and Thomas were also taught how to care for pets growing up, first the goldfish won at the local Gymkhana. Then progressing onto other pets to call their own, although the dogs were always there. Jane had a pet rabbit, called Flopsy, which totally went against the grain with Dad, as wild rabbits are renowned for eating grass and causing problems on the farm. Flopsy was a grey Netherland dwarf, and was gorgeous and loving. The rabbit thing came from the fact that there was an old hutch, that Jane had found in one of the outhouses, that could be done up and repaired. Having a pet growing up is like having a pretend friend, who you can talk too and discuss your problems with, a problem shared and all that. Now Flopsy was a long standing pet and lived with them for nearly 10 years.

Thomas was also a pet lover, but didn't actually have a lot of luck on the pet front. He started off with Hammy, the hamster, who we got from a friend in the village and was brought home in a margarine carton, and placed on the floor, while we watched Neighbours after school. All was well as the hamster couldn't escape the sides, until Mum called "Tea is ready"

Yep you've guessed it, Thomas bounced off the sofa and foot into margarine pot, one squashed hamster! Now this was not funny at the time and the poor hamster didn't survive, but it did teach us to be more careful around animals, and understand that they truly are at our mercy.

Hammy 2 arrived and lived in a converted bird cage, also found in the old outhouse. Not the best plan, as one night he decided to escape and was lost for months in the house! Really not sure how he survived, but he was found months later in the dining room, after Mum nearly stood on him. They all thought that he'd been living behind the skirting boards.

Jane and Thomas also had two white mice at one stage, but they didn't last long! Even thinking about this now gives Jane the shivers, not a mouse lover, unless there is plenty of distance between us, and preferably outside.

The weekend soon came round again, and week one of school was complete. It was starting to get a bit real for Jane as she would be making the move to High School in the following year, with a visit to the open evening. There was no choice of schools when Jane and Thomas were going through the schooling system, so Prudhoe High School it would be. Now Jane's High School days are a whole other story.

As Jane and Thomas were getting older (Middle school age 9-13), they were of much more use to help out at home. So, Dad invariably left the jobs where he needed helpers until weekends, if it wasn't a time sensitive job. They were involved with everything they possibly could be, and soon were quite proficient on a tractor, and useful on the straw and hay stacking.

The annual maintenance of vehicles and machinery started. This was a job Thomas loved getting involved with, mainly as he could get as mucky and oily as possible. Hence Jane and Thomas were always told to wear old clothes that invariably ended up in the bin, or washed to the best of the machines ability and worn again. There was also the maintenance of fences, gates, and troughs - this list is not exhaustive, as there is always something to repair, or replace.

Fencing was fun, as Jane and Thomas used to get a chance to spend time with Dad, while he was working. And giving Mum a well-earned hour or so to herself. Jane and Thomas were useful for running backwards and forwards, fetching and carrying "Can you just.......can you just.....can you just......" Dad would play the game, and as Jane and Thomas got back with one thing, he'd ask for something else. It usually turned into a race to the tractor to retrieve said item, ending in an argument as to who would take it back. Dad soon learnt to ask for two items, Jane was sure half the time he didn't actually need whatever it was, but it kept both Jane and Thomas happy.

School days ticked by, and the days started to get shorter. The summer nights, having field teas, turned into nights, in the garden, catching the last of the sun, sometimes playing a quick game of cricket. The nights soon started to cut in, once the clocks went back, always a weird thing in Jane's mind as a child. She could never actually get her head round what they were actually doing, and then there was the confusing ....well, it would be 4.30pm old time, no there is no old time - it is what time it is now.

Now, obviously most of the devices are electronic and shift automatically to the new time zone, but back then it was like a military operation to get all the clocks on the right time, not to mention the dreaded video recorder clock, because if that wasn't right it would not record the right programme.

Adult Jane would actually giggle out loud to herself at this, as she can picture it so vividly in her mind. Funny how the strangest of things are there in our subconscious, or is it our conscious mind.

Chapter 9

'Tomorrow hopes we have learnt something from yesterday'

-John Wayne

Dad is a true horseman in all ways, and has had ponies and horses in his life, since the day dot. Starting out on a retired pit pony, called "Queenie", there were no quadbikes, or motorbikes, to race around the fields on in those days. For all that the farm consumed most of his time, he always had time for his horses, much to Mum's loathing of the time he spent with them.

Jane spent hours watching Dad groom his horse 'Lady', safely sat in the wire hay rack on the wall, it was a cosy place to be as a toddler, and Lady would often come across and let Jane scratch her nose. It was also a special time to have just Jane and Dad. Once groomed, and the straw bedded down for the night, Dad would ask 'Do you want a sit?' smiling at Jane, as he knew the answer.

Dad would carry Jane on his shoulders and place her gently onto Lady's back.

"You look like a pea on a drum up there." Dad would say every time, then they'd both giggle.

"She's so quiet, I think I could ride her." would be Jane's reply. Looking back now, it just shows we have no fear at that age and Jane was sure Lady was a quiet horse, but does recall some of the states that Dad came home in, after a day out with her.

Jane remembered one day Mum shouting, "What the actual! You aren't coming in here like that. Did you fall off?"

"No, that stupid bloody horse again!" replied Dad, as Jane and Thomas came running to see. He was covered from head to foot in now, dried mud. Jane just couldn't hold in her laughter. "It's alright for you two, just out the bath. I'm frozen to the bone and Lady needs a wash and brush down too" replied Dad.

"Is that your cream jumper under that mud?" Jane asked, she knew fine well, as he wore it all the time under his jacket, cream arran, to keep him warm.

"Yes, it is and my jacket is still around at the loose boxes. It'll have to dry out before I can brush it clean."

"Can I help Dad sort Lady?" Jane asked pleadingly up at Mum.

"Well only if you can be of some help. I think Dad might want a bath to warm up first.

"Once Dad had had his bath and a hot toddy to warm through, they both headed out to the stable. Dad knew Jane was of little to no help, but wanted to tell her the story. Safely positioned in the hay rack, Dad started with a brush, talking softly to Lady. "You silly old girl, you'll never learn..."

Jane started laughing, as Lady was in a right state.

"Well, she won't. Mud is like a magnet. I was just riding along, chatting with Uncle Keith and Phillip, heading for a gateway at the corner of the field. I think it was Uncle Keith that noticed Lady's ears prick up and shouted urgently "Arnold, you'd best get off!!!! He'd seen it happened before, but I wasn't quick enough. It was a like a slow motion movie, and down we went! I managed to jump free before Lady started to roll properly - saddle and all! But this will make you laugh even more, as I ended up tripping over a stone and face planting into the mud anyway. So, we both looked like swamp monsters. Not the most comfortable of ride home I can tell you, but still great fun. Dad winked at Jane.

Jane was nearly asleep, but still smiled back. He picked her up and they walked back round to the house. "Up to bed sleepyhead, I'll see you in the morning" as he kissed Jane goodnight. There was no malice in Lady, but she loved to roll in mud and by gum, if there was a spot, she'd find it.

Now, just imagine Jane's delight when a Shetland Pony arrived. Holly had been a surprise 5th birthday present, and Jane absolutely adored him. It isn't exactly a male name, but Jane had known that's what her pony would be called, before she even had him. Jane spent hours grooming, as Dad had shown her with Lady, and eventually rode not very successfully to start with. Holly was not as quiet as Lady, even though just a third of her size. Dad was in his element, helping Jane and dutifully got Holly tacked up and ready to go.

"Ok missy let's be having you. All ready and waiting." Dad said, pointing to Holly.

A bit apprehensive, Jane wandered over, complete with hard hat and gloves, at least looking the part. Dad gave Jane a leg up, suitably sat straight back and ready to go, they wandered along the yard, so Grandma and Granda could see me.

"Perfect seat." commented Dad, keeping a tight hold of the lead rope. All was well until they turned to head back, and Holly took off at great pace! Dad not able to keep up, he grabbed Jane and let Holly go! Once the shock had worn off and Dad had retrieved Holly, who was head down on the lawn, in front of the house, Shetlands are renowned for being greedy. Jane had to get back on, and off they went again. Jane remembers being absolutely terrified to get back on, but was certainly not a quitter, even at a young age. Once round past the Big House for their second turn, they stopped.

Jane said "I think that's enough for today." Dad nodded and lifted her down, whilst keeping tight hold of Holly. Dad decided he would ride Holly back round to the house, even though his feet were dragging along the ground. Well, you can predict what happened, yes - as soon as Dad hit the saddle, Holly was off like 'a bat out of hell' towards the drying green! Jane hot on their heels, all she saw was a heap of Dad on the top of the yard, rushing up to him.

"You ok Dad, what happened?"

Not the best thing to ask and a lesson learnt, never ask 'What's happened?'

"Stupid beeping pony (or words to that effect), he's thrown me off!" said Dad, with a look of pure rage. He had never been beaten by a pony, or horse, and here they had a Shetland pony, which looked so placid in his field, managing to unseat Jane's Dad. Jane quickly put her hand to her face to cover her smile, which soon broke into laughter and they both laughed.

"I think I'd better spend some time with Holly and try to quieten him down," Dad responded. Well, that never happened, and Jane learnt to ride on Holly, but lead rein only.

Remember, remember the 5th of November. Oh my, Jane and Thomas certainly have some memories of bonfire nights growing up.

Dad had to make sure his horses, and the other animals were safe and happy on 5th, as the loud bangs from the fireworks often frightened them. He checked the horses regularly throughout the night, especially after the display across the river, which the family could watch from the house.

Obviously as toddlers, Jane and Thomas were confined to the house to watch the fireworks from the living room window. Part of the fun for them then was collecting the wood and fallen branches, that had been saved to make the fire, as that meant they could ride in the tractor with Dad, or in the transport box on the back.

Pre bonfire night, there would be a log cutting day, to fill the coal shed with logs, to keep the family warm over the winter, hence the stray branches. It was great fun and a great chance to be at one with nature, all be it with a noisy chainsaw. Jane was sure her and Thomas were more of a hindrance than a help, but fresh air, on a glorious frosty sunny November day is certainly good for you.

"Best let Thomas and me check that there's none of Jimmy mouse's friends about before we start chopping." Jane would say.

"No problem," Dad said, wiping his brow and shaking his head, with a smirk on his face, giving him a chance to have a quick cuppa from his tartan flask, before Jane and Thomas got started.

"Good to go!" shouted Thomas. Dad would cut the logs with Jane and Thomas standing at a safe distance. Inevitably their attention span, and enjoyment of throwing logs into the trailer, waivered after a while and they would explore, climb and just soak up the surroundings. Poor Dad ending up doing most of the work. This certainly didn't happen as Jane and Thomas got older mind, they were told "It's what's going to keep you both warm over the long winter months, so crack on and get throwing."

The coal shed was, in fact, the old Wash House for the Big House, where the servants would wash and dry all the clothing, bedding and anything else that needed cleaning, or washing from the house. Jane didn't actually know a lot about it, but could imagine the hive of activity and the bustle of the workers, singing, gossiping and generally being happy in their work.

Jane and Thomas never realised how lucky they were, with the benefits of technology on their side and how easy their life was. Jane knew that they didn't think it back then. The Wash House was a great place to get lost in the stored bric a brac, in fact this may well have been where the rabbit hutch and bird cage were found. The coal was stored in one side for the family, and Grandma and Granda, to access, with the logs stacked in the other side.

Jane and Thomas would make a guy from an old boiler suit belonging to Dad or Granda, racing round to the hay shed to get straw to stuff it.

"Mind - just the loose bits off the floor," Dad would call after Jane and Thomas as they disappeared round the corner. Mum and Grandma would help Jane and Thomas to tie the legs and sleeves with 'good old baler twine.' As Jane and Thomas grew up, they found 'good old baler twine' had many uses! Jane was sure most farmers will advocate the list is endless and was also sure this will pop up in future tales.

Bonfires started small, with a small fire built at the bottom of the garden. Mam, Dad, Granda, Phil and Irene all there huddled round the fire, in their old coats and woolly hats. Jane often wondered where the fun element was in this, but that was before she realised it was just a good excuse for a knees up, and a chance to socialise, without getting dressed up.

Grandma would sit with Jane and Thomas in the living room window to watch the small fireworks being set off, usually a multi pack bought from Curry's in Prudhoe. They would be carefully placed in a metal shortbread biscuit tin (minus the shortbread) for safety, just in case there were sparks from the fire. As years went by, the fireworks got larger and to be honest, the safety aspect other than a "don't put them too close to the fire, maybe in the cool box would be good" wasn't great, but that's another story! Grandma would join the party, once Jane and Thomas were off to bed and dreaming of the rockets up in the stars.

It did make Jane and Thomas laugh watching Phil and Dad take it in turn to light the blue touch paper and make a run back to a safe distance. Neither Jane nor Thomas were keen on the loud bangs to be honest, but that soon changed as they were allowed to go out and experience the Bonfire night tradition, and the sparklers became a firm favourite. Inevitably this usually turned into a few drinks round the fire. As Jane and Thomas grew, the bonfire grew with them.

The following day was always a slow day in the house, not that Jane and Thomas knew why then, but they soon picked up on the vibe as they got older.

Bonfire night usually signalled the end of half term and a return to school.

"But it won't be long until Christmas," Jane said, as they hopped into the car for another Mum's taxi trip to school.

"Get in!" shouted Thomas "I love Christmas."

"You two are just wishing your lives away. You never realise when you are your age how quickly the years pass as you get older," said Mum, shaking her head "You'll want to cherish every day when you are my age." Jane and Thomas did a wide-eyed owl look at each other and decided to sit in silence until they got to school.

"Don't forget its swimming tonight, so no dawdling, so we can get home and have a quick tea before," shouted Mum as Jane and Thomas jumped out of the car with their briefcases and PE bags.

"PE and swimming in one day isn't good for you." moaned Thomas.

"It is," replied Jane "It's keeping us fit and healthy, and you never know when you might need to save yourself in the water", as she watched him vanish into the distance to meet up with his friends.

Jane wandered aimlessly into school, lost in her own thoughts. Life was starting to get more complicated. Who knew as you got older, life would throw you curved balls to deal with.

It wasn't that Jane hated school, but she was always a bit of a loner, and her friendship group changed and took on new dimensions. Sometimes it was easier just to sit and be happy in her own little world, lost in my imagination. There was no conflict in Jane's imagination - just happiness and a will to be a success at everything she did. Not necessarily competitive, just Jane being a success, probably makes no sense at all, but to 12-year-old Jane it made total sense.

Jane loved sport and this was her release at school, and probably the one thing that got her through school years.

At this time, Jane was probably concentrating on getting good grades, to get into good classes, come the following September, with transition to High School. Whilst most of Jane's friends were excited about this prospect, Jane still had doubts. The High school seemed massive, but then again, the move from First school, to Middle school was huge too.

These thoughts would hold Jane in good stead for future challenges and as it would give her a good ~~an~~ understanding that 'you are you' and that it really doesn't matter what other people think about you or anything that you do, as long as you are happy, and continue to grow into the person that you want to be, and that this will continue throughout your life.

Anyway, Jane had swimming to look forward to, one of her favourite pastimes, once she had mastered staying afloat. Jane wasn't perfect from the off, but had an amazing teacher and as the saying goes, 'took to it like a duck to water'. Badges were soon achieved, and Mum dutifully sewed these onto Jane's swimming costume. She was even entered in for her first swimming gala, a huge achievement. Mum used to watch from the upstairs window in the swimming baths. Jane was sure there was plenty of gossip heard between those four walls on a swim club night. Jane's swim was always celebrated with a packet of green Ringos crisps from the vending machine. It's the simple things.

Days ticked by and the nights started to 'draw' in - Grandma's favourite saying. The fire was lit on a daily basis, and this was a cosy space to spend family time after tea, round the kitchen table. From a young age, it was engrained into Jane and Thomas that tea time was discussion time round the table, with questions on school, what Dad had been doing and planning ahead. These are things that are taken for granted growing up and it is not until later years, that we realise the value of these lessons.

Chapter 10

'Whatever you see frequently, becomes your frequency'

-Brian Cassidy

November moved into December, and the Christmas adverts were a constant reminder that Christmas was just around the corner. The maintenance work of fencing and repairs continued. Dad enjoyed his days out on the horse, and Jane and Thomas had days away with Grandma and Mum.

The Argos and Studio catalogues arrived, and this was a sign that Christmas was approaching.

'Any ideas what you are wanting for Christmas kids?' asked Mum ".

Whoop whoop!" Jane and Thomas both said in unison. They spent hours, with a pen marking their wants, in the books.

Now Christmas time for most people is a time to spend with family and friends, and enjoying the run up to the festivities. Not in the world of little Jane. Jane and Thomas were thankful if school didn't finish until the 22nd of December.

There was always time to fit in a trip to Fenwick's toy fair, to see Father Christmas. There was always a massive queue. Jane can remember standing on the stairs, with Mum and Grandma, trying to pacify Thomas that "it won't be long." It was worth it in the end, as once Jane and Thomas had seen Father Christmas and told him their wish list, they'd spend a good hour in what, as a six-year-old, can only be described as an Aladdin's cave of every toy and game that you could ever imagine including some amazing sledges. The toy fair was the whole top floor of Fenwick's and to Jane and Thomas it was massive. Once they'd dreamed in the toy fair, and seen Father Christmas, they'd go and walk along outside to look at Fenwick's window and enjoy the dream of being in the window storytale displays. Alice in Wonderland is the one that sticks in Jane's mind - how much fun to go into an imaginary world, may be not too far from real life after all. Jane and Thomas' Christmas lists got longer after that visit.

Turkey's, yes turkeys! These arrived in late September, and were housed in the byre around the back of the corn byre, above the cattle for warmth. Jane remembers the pungent smell and the loud gobbling, the weirdest of sounds as she opened the door. An old staircase was used to access the loft and the steps were at a ridiculous angle. Jane had no idea how Dad never fell, especially when he was carrying bags of feed. Turkey time in the run up to Christmas was both stressful and enjoyable. Stressful for Mum and Dad, but enjoyable for Jane and Thomas. They often had a half hour with the plucking team, at a tea break and got the chance to pull out a few feathers, this obviously changed as they got older and were roped in to help.

Now as littlies, there was only so much Jane and Thomas could do. But it did mean that they got to spend time with Grandma and Granda, hearing more stories, and exploring more in the Big House. Jane and Thomas helped to put up the Christmas decorations, which were stored in the cellar, down a stone staircase. Jane had to admit to this day that she never felt comfortable going down into the cellar. It had a smell that can only be described as damp and musty, not the best description, but it's hard to put into words. The main issue was the bricked-up archway, clocked by Jane and Thomas every time that they went down, but neither of them really wanting to know what was behind it. Imagination as a kid is open to all and Jane's imagination was fairly vivid. She can remember thinking that there could be dead bodies and all sorts behind there! Now, as you've probably guessed, there was a story to this, and we all know how Granda like to tell a story. Decorations collected and each with a small bag, Jane and Thomas would climb the stairs back out and into the hallway, amazingly dry as a bone.

“Right let’s start with getting everything organised, then we can have some lunch. I’m making sarnies for the turkey team first, so you can make a start on unpacking.” said Grandma

“Pop the baubles on the stairs and Granda can help you out the robins on the light fittings. I think the tree will be here this afternoon” Grandma bustled along the hall into the kitchen.

“Now then kids before we get started,” said Granda. Jane and Thomas looked at each other knowingly “You’ve no doubt been wondering about the arch in the cellar.”

Yep, Jane and Thomas shook their heads at each other and laughed, “We knew you’d tell us when Grandma wasn’t here.” They giggled, they both loved stories.

“Well, let’s sit on the stairs and I’ll tell you about it” pointed Granda. They all sat in a line along the stairs, there was room for them all and more.

“As far as I know this is true, but you don’t always know the truth, unless it is written down. You both can see the tall chimney stack from your bedroom windows?” Granda asked looking at both Jane and Thomas, checking they were engaged.

“That used to be used as a distillery run by the monks, who ran the farm a long, long time ago. I know it’s hard to believe. Do you know what a monk is?” said Granda.

Jane and Thomas both shook their heads, this was a more in-depth story, nothing like a Jimmy mouse story.

“A monk is someone who dedicates their life to God, the man up there,” Granda pointed up, “in the sky, you’ll understand one day.”

Jane and Thomas were like sponges and just sat taking it all in.

“The monks farmed the land and lived in this house. Now, sometimes things didn’t go their way and as monks, they needed an escape route from any badness. Hence the archway in the cellar, obviously its bricked up now, but that used to be an escape route for them."

Jane and Thomas sat in awe as Granda continued, "Now the underground tunnel was supposedly to the Hall, on the other side of the river. I'm not sure they would manage to build an underground tunnel under the river, so I think it would be to a quiet spot on the river, from where they could row over to the other side."

"Wow, can we knock the bricks down, and see?" said Thomas.

"I think its best they are left where they are, we don't know what we might find behind them." said Granda

"Phew" Jane blew out "I don't think it's a good idea, I get a weird feeling as it is going down there."

And so, the story was born, be it truth or fiction, Jane and Thomas had no idea, but the way Granda told it, they had no reason to believe any different. It is amazing how the mind is acceptant to anything as a child, soaking everything in like a sponge and not worrying if it's actually true or not. We can learn a lot from this and be more open to our marvellous mind as we grow, being open and acceptant, instead of "being set in our ways". We can change our path and create our own journey.

"Lunch is ready!" shouted Grandma.

Jane and Thomas raced along the hallway and positioned themselves at the table. Thomas tucking into his Lurpak butter and sugar sandwich, and Jane into a homemade strawberry jam sandwich, followed by home baked cakes. A sugar rush and some!

Granda liked a snooze after lunch in his rocking chair in the kitchen, so Jane and Thomas left him to it and helped Grandma put up some more decorations. Thomas was straight into the boxes, there was stuff everywhere, but it was great fun.

"I've found what I was looking for." Thomas exclaimed as he came running into the dining room, where Jane and Grandma were putting some freshly cut holly around the light fittings. Holding up the snow house "There's nothing in it though?" he questioned.

"That's because Father Christmas fills it on Christmas Eve." explained Grandma.

"Ah I see, so he comes here too?" asked Thomas.

"Of course," replied Grandma "You can check when you come for tea on Christmas day. Julie and Jamie are coming too." smiled Grandma.

"Get in, that'll be fun, I can't wait." Thomas replied excitedly.

"There's still lots to do before then mind, so we'll have to keep moving." Grandma said patting him on the back.

They soon had all the decorations up and were sat in the kitchen making more paper chains, complete with glue sticks and glitter.

All of a sudden there was a honk of a horn and the dogs went flying to the back door.

"That'll be Harry" said Grandma dashing off to find her purse. Jane and Thomas looked up from the decorations and raised their eyebrows. They jumped down from the table, complete with glittered hands and, more than likely, clothes too and headed in the same direction as the dogs. Harry was the driver of the Longstaff's baker van that came every week. The family were the last stop, so Jane and Thomas knew it was treat time, as did the dogs. Funny how we are creatures of habit and soon learn a routine. Harry was great and always kept a Victoria sponge cake for the family. Even though Grandma made an amazing sponge, you couldn't beat a bakery cake. There was often a "spare" chocolate éclair and peach melba too, an extra treat.

As the turkey pluckers finished up for the night, it usually took 2-3 days to get them all de feathered and hung ready to "dress". Grandma would bring Jane and Thomas home and have them bathed, and in front of the fire, ready for bed when Mum and Dad came in. Tomorrow was another day of turkey, but this was fetch and carry day, once they were dressed in the dairy, they were carried round to the old empty cottage, weighed and sorted ready for people to collect. Now writing that down it all sounds so simple, but nothing in this life is simple, as we all know.

This was all going on whilst school plays, school Christmas parties were attended and Jane's heightened joy of the Christmas period reached high fever pitch. Not an easy time for any of us.

As with lambing time, Jane and Thomas were in charge of the wheelbarrow, to get the turkeys from the dairy to the cottage, well for some of the time. Lined with a clean sheet, they stacked the turkeys in and would push them round to the cottage, where Mum would weigh them. Then a ticket was added, with a number on to the leg, added to a list and put in on paper lined trestle tables. Invariably, there were disasters, but the family laughed about it and kept going. It was good to get the chatter from the helpers in the dairy and be involved.

Jane and Thomas knew to make a sharp exit on the evening, when Mum and Dad sat down, to try and sort out who was getting what!

"There isn't enough 15lb ones. There are a few with bruises and there are no 18lb birds!" The list was endless.

Jane was sure Mum and Dad had many a sleepless night in the run up to Christmas. There was also the added stress of the value of the turkeys, and the amount of time and effort to get to this stage. Over the years, the family had various home security systems in place - from the tractor being parked across the old cottage doorway, to the old baby intercom!

The old cottage was a fabulous place to store the turkeys, as it was totally run down and could be cleaned easily and, as there was no heating system, it was cool storage. Jane and Thomas spent hours playing house in there and using their imagination to create the perfect home. The smell of Zoflora from the old pantry, and the green glass bottle of air freshener on the windowsill, is still a vivid memory in Jane's mind. Jane and Thomas found all sorts of treasures, well things that they thought were treasures.

Once the list was complete, Mum liked to check that the turkey allocated to the person, would meet expectations. Not Dad's favourite time as there was always a fall out.

"You two want to come across to Gary's, to deliver his turkeys?" Dad shouted, Gary is an old friend of Dad's, who owns a butcher's shop and who had a turkey order from the family every year. Poor Gary often got the bruised birds or torn skins.

"Yep, we'll help you load up the car too" Jane shouted back.

Once loaded, they headed off.

"Can we get pies for tea?" Thomas asked, "I'd say so," Dad replied.

Jane and Thomas played their Christmas music cassette much to Dad's irritation, but he smiled and sang along.

Turkeys dropped, and a goody bag of all sorts collected, they headed home. Mum was dealing with people collecting their turkeys. It was a busy day and there was a lot of laughter and conversation. There was always one, or two people, who left it until the last minute to collect and Dad would bring their turkeys into the house, so he didn't have to make the trip across to the cottage. Once all the turkeys were safely off to their Christmas homes, Mum and Dad would breathe a huge sigh of relief, and the family Christmas could start.

Chapter 11

"Why, sometimes I've believed as many as six impossible things before breakfast."

Alice in Wonderland – Lewis Caroll

It was a mad rush to get the house decorated for Christmas day once the turkeys had all been collected. No putting the tree up in November! Dad was armed with the outside lights to go round the trees in the garden, while Mum, Jane and Thomas did the tree in the dining room. Complete with all their homemade decorations.

Christmas Eve soon came around and this was a traditional trip across to see Gran and Granda Ben. An amazing tea with the family. Dad is one of three brothers and Gran ~~is~~ was one of eight, so you can imagine arriving in the yard at Colepike Farm and cars abandoned in every space possible. Brothers, sisters, partners, kids a plenty. This was a magical time for us kids, running round and no one cared. Auntie Gertie, Granda Ben's sister, was in her element, with her large tea pot topping up the teacups. Homemade everything and chattering that could compete with a football match crowd.

Once tea was complete, everyone mucked in to carry plates and cups to the kitchen, the big tidy took what seemed like minutes. 'Many hands make light work' and how true that is, although the children were out of the way in the living room, fire roaring, enjoying the crackers from the Christmas tree.

Uncle Ronnie clapped loudly twice "Right folks, let's get this show on the road. Lillian start the music." Dutifully Auntie Lillian opened up the piano and started playing Silent Night, soon everyone was in the living room voices tuned and ready for action. Auntie Lillian played on, Good King Wenceslas was the cue to get hats and coats on. In convoy, everyone set off in cars, often arguments as to who was going with who, on with the carol singing.

The family all headed a mile or so down the road to what can only be described as an awesome house, with a huge front door. A massive Christmas tree, from floor to ceiling, centred at the foot of the grand staircase. As a kid to Jane, this was like a dream home that you could imagine yourself living in as a grown up. The owners requested their carols, and everyone sang their hearts out. Many pound notes were placed in the charity pots and they moved to onto the village green for the carol service, beautiful.

Tired and usually cold, the family headed home to get ready for Father Christmas. A little cat nap on the journey home had Jane's batteries recharged for a short period, to get the plate of treats and a tody put on the dining room table for Father Christmas. Oh, and the carrots and corn for Rudolph at the back door.

"Don't forget to make sure the fire is out before you come to bed, mind." Thomas pointed as they headed up to bed, hearts racing in excitement for the following day and what might be under the tree waiting for them. Jane never had any problems going to sleep on Christmas Eve, as the fresh, and playing with Catherine and Alison, had worn her out. Jane and Thomas enjoyed Dad reading T'was the night before Christmas to them just before they dropped off into their dreamy sleep.

Christmas Day dawned............

Now most kids are up with the larks on Christmas Day, not Jane and Thomas, who weren't early risers - although Dad might say otherwise?

Jane and Thomas would sneak into each other's room, wait, and giggle with excitement, trying to decide whether Mum and Dad were awake, or whether to wait a bit longer. Jane and Thomas would eventually run along the landing when they felt brave enough, burst into Mum and Dad's bedroom and shout "Happy Christmas Day!!!" Closely followed by "Do you think Father Christmas has been?" Flying down the stairs as fast as their little legs would carry them, with Mum and Dad hot on their heels.

Bingo!! Father Christmas had been and left all Jane and Thomas' presents next to the tree. It was so magical, and Jane's memories come flooding back. Over the years Jane can recall a rather large cuddly panda, that was nearly as big as her, that she had spotted in Fenwick's toy fair (obviously she didn't make the link at the time). A cabbage patch kid, Sindy doll, with horse and caravan, Jane wasn't a Barbie girl. Thomas was obviously all for farming kit, tractors, farm animals and the good old sit on tractor that Jane and Thomas spent hours on. There were always games too - Hungry hippos being a favourite, Jaws, Buckaroo and, of course, Trivial Pursuit - that nobody could answer the questions too, to get the pie!

"I'll have to pop out and check the stock, but won't be long." said Dad. The animals still need caring for on Christmas Day, they don't have a day off. A farmer lives for the farm and it's a 24/7 365 day job, but if you speak to any farmer, they wouldn't have it any other way. It's a life they choose and a way of life, not a job. Some may say not always, but Jane was sure that in their hearts, it is.

"Right, we need to get sorted to go along to the Big House for lunch. Pop the things you want to take in a pile and Dad will take it over when he gets in" said Mum. Well, that was a bit like a military operation because Jane and Thomas didn't really want to leave anything behind. But Mum knew that there would be more along the yard, so ultimately things got left, and Jane and Thomas never missed them.

All sorted, and dressed in their posh clothes for the lunch, the family tootalled along the yard and burst into the Big House. "Happy Christmas" rang out from all directions, big hugs, and kisses. A fabulous smell of turkey and all the trimmings. The kitchen table was overflowing with goodies. How they ever got through it all was beyond Jane, but there was never much left.

"Has Santa been here?" asked Thomas. Granda winked at him and tickled his chin, then reaching across to Jane, and looking at them both said, "Now, before we get comfy in the dining room, I want you both to put your hands over your eyes."

Granda continued, "I'm going to walk you to the hall door, no peeping mind." Jane and Thomas both looked and smiled, and quickly slapped their hands over their eyes. The hall door was opened, "whooo hoo" Jane and Thomas cheered as they dropped their hands and dashed along the hallway.

"This is amazing", closely followed by "How did Santa get this down the chimney?" - this was met with great hilarity from the grownups. Jane and Thomas were soon at the top of the huge slide that filled the hallway, and were nearly able to reach the top of the Christmas tree.

"Yeah ha" they screamed, as they flew to the bottom. "Now we have to navigate round this all day" said Grandma shaking her head "God help us when Julie and Jamie arrive for teatime".

The dining room, with its huge table, was all set, complete with red tablecloth, and all the posh knives and folks. The food was carried from the kitchen, and everyone tucked into a fabulous Christmas lunch, turkey carved by Granda, making a big show of sharpening his knife. Once lunch was complete, rounded off with trifle, it was time to show off all the presents, and just enough time before the teatime rabble arrived. Mum and Grandma reorganised the dining room, extra chairs, the winding handle on the table to add in the extra leaf, new tablecloth and the tea set out of the huge oak dresser.

Auntie Margaret, Uncle Peter, Julie, and Jamie arrived mid-afternoon, closely followed by Uncle Ronnie and Auntie Edith. It was a re-run of Easter really. Family time is precious, even though we never realise when we are younger. In fact, there was, more often than not, a lot of whinging from the children about the time spent travelling to visit family. Jane is grateful now for this time and have wonderful memories of her childhood.

Uncle Ronnie loved to play games master, and this is where he came into his own. Once he'd had a good puff on his pipe, he would pull a whistle from his pocket, one long blast and everyone jumped to attention. Sat in the bay window in the wingback chair, he'd say, "Are you ready? Are you ready? Then let the games commence,"

With the games master in place, and a roaring fire going in the drawing room, everyone shared laughs, enjoyed the new games and obviously fell out, all over a period of time. Jane and Thomas had no concept of time at that age. Whilst they were busy playing - Grandma, Auntie Edith, Auntie Margaret, and Mum were busy creating an evening feast in the dining room. How anyone never popped from the amount of food consumed, Jane had no idea.

All round the table for tea. Jane says tea - there was everything you could ever imagine, or dream of, complete with Lurpak, and sugar sandwiches for Thomas. Crackers pulled and hats on, jokes told, and teacups charged. It was laughter aplenty and more pretending playing house. Jane and Julie loved the mini tea sets in the dresser and went round asking people if they would like more tea. Now fuelled with a sugar over dose, the last of the surprises for the day - the Santa house,filled with lots of little gifts, the final excitement for the day.

Tired and weary, Jane and Thomas would head home along the yard. Sometimes being carried and popped straight into bed.

Christmas is a special time of year, and the memories Jane holds fill her with joy. There are many more and this is just a snapshot of her early years.

The Christmas holidays were a time to recharge for Mum and Dad, following the pressure of the turkeys beforehand. Jane and Thomas were often left to their own devices, playing games, organising their new Christmas toys, falling out - which happened regularly, and generally running riot.

Friends often came to visit from the village and if there was a snowstorm, Jane and Thomas were straight out with sledges - friends and all. The best place to sledge was down the side of the house, sometimes resulting in hitting a hedge! They were always accompanied by Dad, on the pink sledge, as it was fast. Dad had his uses, like pulling Jane and Thomas back to the top of the hill, or even carrying Thomas over his shoulder in a fertiliser bag, they were a great alternative to a sledge. Jane is sure that there will be movie footage, taken on the old super 8 movie camera. How no one ended up with broken bones, Jane will would never know.

More often than not, they were joined by Phil and Irene, pre Michael years, obviously. Ultimately, it turned out to be a fun day of races, their version of snowboard cross on sledges. The day would come to an end when Dad had to feed up and check the animals. The children would all retire to the house to sit in front of the warm fire, with a hot chocolate and Mum's millionaire shortbread.

It was quite a hike back up to the village for their friends, and often the bank wasn't safe for cars to travel down. So, Dad was often roped in, to give them a ride home on the tractor. They were always super excited by this idea, and talked about it at school non-stop. There seemed to be more snow when Jane was small, or maybe that's just because she was small and there looked like more.

New Year's Eve signalled that the school holidays were nearly over. But this was another gathering of the masses. This time at Jane and Thomas' house, with merriment from the outset. For future reference, when Phil and Irene, from the bungalow, were involved in anyway, shape or form, it was guaranteed to be a fun filled day, or night, or in some cases, both!

"Who hoo!" came a voice from the backdoor. It was Irene "In here." shouted back Mum.

Jane's mind was ticking, as too little Jane these grownups all seemed to be a lot older that the children, but in fact, they were younger than Jane is now. Making Jane feel ancient.

With glasses charged, and the record player going as loud as it possibly could, the dancing round the Christmas tree and singing would start. Then Jane and Thomas would quickly be ushered to bed by Grandma. The party would continue until the early hours, as per any party hosted at Jane and Thomas' childhood home.

Once again, the 1st of January would be a slow day, unless Dad had a day out on the horse planned. This meant an early start to feed up and get Lady ready, then, off to meet Uncle Keith and Phillip. It was soon time to take down the Christmas decorations and pack them into the boxes, ready for next year. This was always a downer of a day, as it meant tidying away toys, but as kids, Jane and Thomas were lucky to have a whole room, the playroom, at the end of the house. So, the toys that they'd marked down in the catalogue, and looked at in wonder on the television adverts, and delivered by Father Christmas, were added to the heap of other things in the playroom. All the excitement gone from Christmas in a flash. The huge slide took centre stage inside, until it could be put in the garden in the spring.

The dream and desire for the toy, or game, far outweighing the actual toy itself. Now that sounds quite deep and ungrateful. Jane was never ungrateful for the gifts received, and dreams did come true. Father Christmas was a magical time for Jane and Thomas as children, and Jane is eternally grateful for the pains that Dad, Mum, and Grandma went through to make their dreams come true.

Jane believes that Grandma was actually deposited at the top of Northumberland Street, early one morning, to join a very long queue at Fenwick's, to purchase her cabbage patch doll, which takes pride of place even now on top of her wardrobe.

Just like Alice in Wonderland, it is the dream and imagination that keeps you focused in life, and growing into the person you want to be.

Chapter 12

'Peeling the layers of an Onion – we are never done.'

-Brian Cassidy

The Christmas holidays were always the shortest holidays in the school calendar, and you no sooner were in the build up to Christmas, then the usual…

"Early night tonight kids. It's back to school tomorrow. I hope you've had a great Christmas holiday. You need to get your uniforms sorted out, so there's no panic stations in the morning" said Mum, with a look of relief on her face, no doubt looking forward to a lazy day tomorrow.

"Start of another full term and my exams for High school" said Jane, huffing and puffing.

"Not sure what we'll be doing. All I do know is it's cross country in PE and that's not exactly my favourite pass time, do you think I can be excused somehow?" Thomas questioned.

"I'm sure Mrs Robson will be pleased to see a strapping lad like you take on the challenge" winked Dad.

"Aye well, I might just walk round and soak in the surroundings. You can see quite a bit of farming activity from the school." replied Thomas.

They all laughed, and Mum ushered them upstairs to get organised for tomorrow.

"You two moving up there" Mum's regular Monday morning call, always slightly louder following a holiday. Mum, getting no response, was soon banging on Jane and Thomas' bedroom doors. "You've got 15 minutes. I am going to start the car in the garage. Chop chop, God waits for no man!"

Jane and Thomas heard her footsteps bounding down the stairs.

Morning soon dawned.

Jane had been lying awake in bed, just not wanting to move, exams praying on her mind, she needed to do well in these, to make sure that she was in good classes on moving up to the High school, no pressure then. She so wished she was less of a worrier, always over thinking. Neither Jane or Thomas had time to have breakfast, grabbed their briefcases and out to the car, which was nice and toasty.

And so, another term of school was started, not long until the February half term, six weeks and 3 days, not that Jane was counting. Dad waved them off at the veranda of the Big House, as he was coming back in from leading hay out to the sheep.

Winter is about feeding, and nurturing, the livestock through the tough days of snow, frost, wet spells and whatever else is thrown at them. During the last week, there had been snow on the ground, so Dad had been putting hay out to all the sheep, so they had something to eat. Jane had helped during the holidays, and especially enjoyed doing the turnip feeding, from the transport box on the back of the tractor, for the sheep. Dad had even let Jane have a go driving the tractor, while he threw out the turnips. They hadn't told Thomas, it was their little secret, he wouldn't be impressed. The sheep loved the turnips, and formed an orderly queue behind the tractor, rushing over to leave the hay already spread out for them. If you concentrated, you could make some great sheep lines! Jane managed once to make a heart shape of sheep. Maybe it was her creative streak coming out, it wasn't the best and Dad was certainly confused, and also worried that Jane was losing control of the tractor, but he was suitably impressed when it was finished. No mobile phones in those days to take a snap, so just the snap in Jane's memory.

The days ticked over, and the weeks of winter passed, with Jane and Thomas helping at weekends. They even got the odd trip out for fish and chips at Seahouses, or a wander around at

Wallington Hall. All this, once Dad had done his daily feeding, Mum had milked Bangers and Mash, had Penny out for a walk and all the various other jobs that needed to be done, before a day out could start.

The days are short in the winter months, and there is nothing better than sitting in the cosy living room, in front of a roaring open fireplace. A Sunday afternoon, the family were often found relaxing like this, once the traditional Sunday Roast had been devoured, the trays of Yorkshire puddings just kept coming out. The TV was usually on in the background, sometimes they would play games, and laugh and carry on, but Dad did enjoy a snooze after his lunch, so Jane and Thomas went to play in the playroom at the other end of the house, so as not to disturb the snoozing.

This was their space and great fun, even if it looked a bit like a bomb site, with stuff everywhere. Jane and Thomas were also allowed to draw and paint on the walls, again allowing Jane's creativity to flow. Some of her masterpieces could well be hidden under the current wallpaper! Jane says master pieces, as that's what she thought they were, at the time.

Thomas had his farm set up in a corner of the room, and would spend hours moving corn in trailers, loading sheep and cows, and moving them around fields – a true farmer at heart. Jane and Thomas sent teddy bears down the big slide, chased each other, shouted at each other, and basically enjoyed their time together in this space. Jane and Thomas were extremely lucky to have each other, making Jane aware that you never realise this at the time.

Dad would awake from his slumber and head out to do the evening jobs. Mum would milk the goats and get tea organised. It was a Sunday night ritual to watch Ski Sunday, toasting crumpets on the open fire, laden with butter and syrup, careful not to burn them on the toasting forks. Dreaming of being an awesome skier and being able to venture down the slopes at that speed, and compete at this level, was a pipe dream.

Having recently returned from a school trip to Chatel in France, Jane honestly thought that this was something that she could do, not understanding that it's so much easier to be a good skier if you live where you can train regularly, but you have to dream, don't you. Dream big and your dreams will come true.

Sunday teatime soon became Monday morning and the weekly school runs continued for Mum. The weather started to improve and frosty mornings, with glorious sunshine soon brightened Jane and Thomas spirits with the thought of Spring being just around the corner.

Frosty walks with Grandma, Mum and Penny were just the best, soaking in the sunshine and watching nature at its best, starting to wake from the winter sleep. Jane loved to watch the first signs of Spring, with the green shoots of the snowdrops starting to push through the soil, their tender shoots sometimes pushing up through a late snowfall. In no time, there is a magical show of delicate white bells, hanging their heads and creating a carpet of white in the gardens and hedgerows. To Jane, they are the symbol of new beginnings, and the start of a new cycle in the farming calendar.

February half term was spent getting the shed ready to bring in the ewes, ready for lambing time. Moving hay and straw, erecting gates, and troughs, washing buckets and generally sorting out the lambing spaces. Mucking out the little pens that might need to be used. 'All hands on deck', while Dad had extra help.

"Get your wellies on and we'll head out to ~~and~~ feed the sheep in the pens, to help out Dad" said Mum, as we pulled the car into the garage, after another day at school.

That, reader, is the start of a whole new cycle of life on the farm. New life on the farm in the form of lambs, and the whole farming year unfolds, year on year, as Jane grows - farming life grows around her, with the added responsibilities that challenge us along the way. Life moves on, and the outside world continues to tick on, as we grow from the inside out.

The cycle of farming life continues..................

Back to reality, and to the here and now, life is now, now is all we have.

"Oh my" said Jane, to Bella and Mollie "I really can't believe what I have achieved these last 7 weeks, can you?" Obviously, the dogs couldn't answer back, but Mollie was wagging her tail and throwing the tennis ball up in the air, whilst Bella looked lovingly into Jane's eyes, as if they knew exactly what she was rambling on about.

It was a glorious sunny morning. The sun was shining, and Jane had even put her shorts on! Not quite flip flop weather, but we can live in hope. That would be handy, in time for lambing. It was a total contrast to the wet and miserable morning at the start. The daffodils were starting to flower, the grass was growing, and most importantly, the sun had put a smile on Jane's face.

"Well, I've only gone and written a book. I know that you didn't think I could" Jane said to no one in particular, but looking up into the deep blue sky, peppered with fluffy clouds.

Life throws spanners in the works for everyone, and sometimes you have to embrace the chance to reset and grasp an opportunity to express yourself, as the true person you are. This is Jane's time to fully express her desire, and dreams, and increase her awareness of how life can be good again, if she can be the "me" that she wants to be.

'Thoughts become things. If you can see it in your mind, you can hold it in your hand'

-Bob Proctor

Author's Note

The story of *Janey – You Never Realise* is based on my life, in the early years, growing up on the family farm. Whilst this book is based on my memories of growing up, I am well aware that there will be some anomalies, and for that, I am using my artistic licence.

I thank you, my reader, for taking the time to read this, my debut book and I am blown away by the support that I have received from family and friends, both old and new, to continue this dream and make it a reality.

If you have enjoyed this book and want to be kept up to date with more of Janey's adventure's as she travels through life, drop me a note.

email: janeaanderson1@gmail.com

Facebook: Jane Anderson

Instagram: jane_a_anderson

LinkedIn: Jane Anderson

Quotes from Janey 'You Never Realise'

'Field Tea'

'You never realise'

'You Two moving up there?'

'Get your wellies on'

'Jimmy Mouse and friends'

'It's the journey and who you become'

-Ciaran Deaney

'If it's not planted properly, it won't grow'

-Brian Cassidy

'If you think you can't, think that you can. Your thinking is the only thing stopping you'

-Ciaran Deaney

'Start to dream big, think beyond possibilities. Our power is in the now'

-Kim Calvert

"Smell the sea and feel the sky. Let your soul and spirit fly."

-Van Morrison

'It is what it is! And it will be what it is'

-Brian Cassidy

'Don't judge each day by the harvest you reap, but by the seeds you plant. Harvest the good and forget the rest'

-Brian Cassidy

'Just because you think it doesn't mean it's true. Whatever you think today creates tomorrow'

-Ciaran Deaney

'If I wanna be free, I gotta be me. You are you're only problem; you are your own solution'

-Brian Cassidy

'Tomorrow hopes we have learnt something from yesterday'

-John Wayne

‘Whatever you see frequently, becomes your frequency’

-Brian Cassidy

‘Why, sometimes I've believed as many as six impossible things before breakfast. ‘

Alice in Wonderland – Lewis Caroll

‘Peeling the layers of an Onion – we are never done.’

-Brian Cassidy

Acknowledgements

Now I will forget at least one person, probably more, that should be included in this section. I am not as young as I used to be and if I don't have a go to list, I am in no man's land. If I happen to have forgotten to add you to my list, I do apologise it has been a rollercoaster and is certainly not intentional. So, for all those that I might have missed and think they should be here I sincerely thank you for whatever you have done.

I have dreamt of writing a book for years and without the support of family and friends, both old and new this would still very much be where it was in a dream. So here goes, to the people who have inspired, helped, listened to me whinge, given me snippets to add and most of all supported me in writing my first book I thank you from the bottom of my heart you are all amazing.

Jo Oliver for introducing me to Brian Cassidy at Dynamite Lifestyle, I now know why I travelled into Newcastle on a cold November night trying to get parked when our beloved Newcastle United were playing at home. I certainly wouldn't be stressing as much now as my car park space would just be. Brian Cassidy for believing in me and chatting at me for a good half hour so I could believe in me and start on the journey. Ann Gundi for introducing me to my amazing book coach Mirav Tarka. The AA club in Lanzarote (you know who you are) for giving me the confidence to continue in my quest and keep writing. Thomas Harrison for being you! You laughed when I said I was doing this, but I hope I can make you cry with joy. Kim Calvert of Dynamite Lifestyle for being the most amazing mentor. Arnold Harrison aka Dad keeping me right on the farming side, being up in the hills for 23 years my memory has slipped a bit as to how the farmers in the 'land of milk and honey' do it.

A Mahoosive shout out to Mirav Tarka aka my book coach who I am proud now to call a friend. Without you this would, most certainly have still been a pipe dream. You have nurtured me, given me tools I never even thought I would need and most of all been a friendly bright red smile once a week to keep me motivated. All virtually through the power of the universe. You have not only helped me write my first book, but you have also helped me grow into the me I want to be.

To my very patient cover designer, Natasa Ivancevic it is outstanding and just how I imagined it to be.

My editor extraordinaire Hilary Norton who has kindly given up her time to edit my raw writing, not an easy task but she has embraced each chunk and helped create the book you are reading today. Julie Wilson for being the final proofread before publishing. We knew you would find some tweaks.

Last and by no means least Charlotte and James my two rocks who have had to make their own tea on occasions, so this book got to be published by the deadline. You are both amazing young adults and I am so proud of you both, not once have you doubted me.

To each and every one of you who have read or been involved in any shape or form to make the dream come true, I am so happy and grateful to have you all.

With much love and gratitude

Jane ♥

About the Author

Jane is starting out on her personal journey as an author, she is discovering the power of the mind and the energy and vibration of life.

With the support of her Dynamite Lifestyle family, her book coach Mirav Tarka, supportive family and friends both old and new, she has achieved her first goal. Following the trials and trauma of the past two years her debut book 'Janey You Never Realise' has been published.

Jane is from the hills of Northumberland, near the Scottish Border in the UK. Jane moved north from her family farm in the Tyne Valley when she married her soul mate Jonathan, she continues to embrace the hills, open space and the tranquillity it has to offer, which is a total contrast to the farm life where she grew up.

She is a very proud Mum of two teenagers Charlotte and James who are starting out on their journey of life.

Jane is often found getting her vitamin D fix in the garden or walking her four-legged friends Bella and Mollie. As soon as the sun makes an appearance the shorts and flip flops are dusted down.

Book Club Questions

What was your favourite part of the book?

Who was the most empowering character?

What did you learn about farm life?

Did you resonate with any of the characters?

- If so who and why?

Did the book make you feel part of farm life?

- If yes, which part impacted you the most?

Did the book make you want to know more? If yes, about what?

Would you recommend this book to other people?

If you are not a member of the book club email me your thoughts at janeaanderson1@gmail.com as an author it is always good to receiver feedback

Janey

Janey

Janey

Janey

Janey

Janey

Janey

Printed in Great Britain
by Amazon